Archive, Slow Ideology and Egodocuments as Microhistorical Autobiography

This book aims to demonstrate how scholars in recent times have been utilizing egodocuments from various angles and providing an opening for the multivocality of the sources to be fully appreciated. The first part of the book is concerned with the significance of egodocuments, both for the individual him/herself who creates such documents, and also for the other, who receives them. The author approaches the subject on the basis of his own personal experience, and goes on to discuss the importance of such documents for the academic world, emphasizing more general questions and issues within the fields of historiography, philosophy of history, microhistory, and memory studies. The second part of the book is based upon a photographic collection – an archive – that belonged to the author's grandfather, who over decades accumulated photographs of vagabonds and outsiders. This part seeks to explore what kind of knowledge can be applied when a single source – an archive, document, letter, illustration, etc. – is examined, and whether the knowledge derived may not be quite as good in its own context as in the broader perspective.

Sigurður Gylfi Magnússon is Professor of Cultural History and chair of the Department of History at the University of Iceland. He is also chair of the Center for Microhistorical Research.

T0347167

Archive, Slow Ideology and Egodocuments as Microhistorical Autobiography

Potential History

Sigurður Gylfi Magnússon

Routledge
Taylor & Francis Group

NEW YORK AND LONDON

First published 2022
by Routledge
605 Third Avenue, New York, NY 10158

and by Routledge
2 Park Square, Milton Park, Abingdon, Oxon, OX14 4RN

Routledge is an imprint of the Taylor & Francis Group, an informa business

Library of Congress Cataloging-in-Publication Data
A catalog record for this title has been requested

ISBN: 978-1-032-01079-3 (hbk)
ISBN: 978-1-032-01196-7 (pbk)
ISBN: 978-1-003-17766-1 (ebk)

DOI: 10.4324/9781003177661

Typeset in Times New Roman
by KnowledgeWorks Global Ltd.

In memory of
my grandfather
Helgi Magnússon
blacksmith and merchant, Reykjavík
b. 8 May 1872, d. 13 March 1956
and
my father
Magnús Helgason
managing director, Reykjavík
b. 24 November 1916, d. 5 October 2000

Contents

Note

* In brackets in the list of contents are the names written on the back of
each photograph in the handwriting of my grandfather, Helgi Magnússon. No attempt has been made to verify their identities. The names are
included here simply as a matter of interest.

Episode I

1 The Book

The 'Slow' Process of Historical Analysis

One man

Gvendur *dúllari* (Chanting Gvendur) alone in the middle of nowhere with all his worldly possessions bundled up in underwear and tied to his chest – far away from anyone else. How could that be? Probably he was the oddity to whom we generally pay little attention. No time or place was focused on Chanting Gvendur. He was alone.

DOI: 10.4324/9781003177661-1

A photograph of one man.

Yet Chanting Gvendur had one friend, none other than Símon *Dalaskáld* (the Dalir poet). A renowned Italian scientist made a study of their relationship and discovered that they used a unique form of sign language. It was like none other – yet effectively served the needs of both men in the societal niche where they existed.

Chanting Gvendur's good fortune lay in other people's conviction that he existed without context – alone in the middle of nowhere.

A photograph of one man.

My Grandfather and His Way of Approaching Life

For a long time I did not understand why my grandfather collected photographs of strangers; I could not see the point of it, and was quite unable to fathom this passion.

In 1999, an Icelandic publishing house decided to invite scholars at the Reykjavík Academy and some of the authors on its list to select a photograph and write something about it. The results would be published in book form. I was at that time chair of the Reykjavík Academy, and I was keen to be part of the project; I knew immediately what photograph I would choose. It was from my grandfather's collection: a photograph of a man known as 'Rat' Petersen.

The text I wrote about 'Rat' Petersen would be the beginning of something more: at that point I understood the value of the photographs; I felt I grasped, to some extent, my grandfather's motivation better than before. That was at the time when the *grand narrative* approach to history was on the brink of collapse; its importance, at least, was greatly reduced, and many scholars within the humanities started to consider where their research stood in the scholarly context.[1] That process sparked a development in my thinking as a historian which opened my eyes to the opportunities my grandfather's photographs offered. I started writing about more of the pictures, which in due course formed the backbone of the book *Snöggir blettir* (*Soft Spots*), published in Icelandic in 2004 – on which part of this book is to some extent based.[2]

Soft Spots takes account of one aspect of the 'Slow' ideology, although the Slow concept is not specifically addressed in the book. In it I explore the circumstances which imbued with meaning the 'soft spots' in people's personalities. The book is fiction from start to finish: a historian's fiction, grounded in my feel for the subject, and the approach I deemed necessary in order to display the conclusions I had reached – conclusions which must be adjudged quite unscientific, but fall within the framework of what microhistorians call the 'evidential paradigm.' I cast the book in the form of autobiography, a form I have been working with in the scholarly context in recent years, in the field of egodocuments. This approach is something I prefer to call 'Potential History,' that will be explained later in the book.

This *non*-autobiography is based upon the above-mentioned photographic collection of my grandfather, Helgi Magnússon, who over decades accumulated photographs of vagabonds and outsiders, individuals who were well known in Icelandic society for their unconventional lifestyles and behavior. The collection grew over the years to be quite considerable. My father, Magnús Helgason, told me that Grandfather Helgi had been in the habit of sitting over his collection for hours, and enjoyed leafing through the pictures. This 'archive' was passed on to me in 1980, at the time when I was commencing my history studies at university. My father probably saw it as appropriate that the pictures should be committed to my care, since I was pursuing such study; he himself had an interest in the Icelandic 'local tale tradition' and drew no firm distinction between such informal learning and formal historical scholarship.

My idea for the book (apart from my obvious personal perspective on my grandfather's 'archive') was quite simply to explore what kind of knowledge can be applied when a single source – an archive, document, letter, illustration, etc. – is examined, and whether the knowledge derived may not be as good in its own context as in the broader perspective. This methodological experiment of the book was assuredly part of my microhistorical development and approach, especially that which compels the scholar to scrutinize the subjective context, temper the researcher's grandiosity, slow down the research process and give oneself time to consider factors which generally make no impression on the person analyzing and exploring. In that sense the text of this book is an improvisation based on the materiality of the photographs and the effects they produce. Guided by such ideas, I write this book, placing myself within the framework laid out in it. One could argue that I draw not only from my microhistorical focus, but also from my scholarly engagement with the history of emotions.[3] This time I myself and my ancestry are in the spotlight, instead of unrelated people from past centuries.

My discussion of the photographs is framed to resemble conventional chapters of autobiographies, which I have connected together by invented letters: one supposed to have been written by my grandfather to my father on his birthday, November 24, 1938, when he was a student in Berlin; another purportedly written to me by my father on the same date in 1993, when I was a doctoral student in the US; and a letter I imagined writing to the future, once again on November 24, in the year 2000, shortly after my father's death. All the letters are 'true' in the subjective sense, based on collective family memory.

Soft Spots, as presented in this book, is an ode to certain conditions that go to shape the world – possibly peripheral cultures, or the boundary between different worlds. Which individuals find themselves excluded? And what is the contribution of people in that situation to the society which in some sense rejects their existence? What is the relationship between scholarship and people in this context? What is the impact of researchers' priorities on our perception of society? I realized that this particular archive offered me the opportunity to consider the above-mentioned questions, and on entirely different terms from my previous work.

What have we in the present day lost of the vision of such individuals, who lived between different cultural worlds? Their perspective clearly differed from that of the majority of their contemporaries, and their interpretation of such concepts as freedom, justice, time and speed was unlike that of those who pursued a conventional bourgeois life – those who were constantly hurrying from A to B, and whose philosophy of life would lead the way to fast food, freeways and modern consumerism.

Some of this seems to have made its impression on my grandfather, that pillar of the community, who apparently gave it some thought in his own quiet manner. For myself, on the other hand, I did not properly grasp the importance of the pictures until I walked one day down a corridor of the Reykjavík Academy and contemplated large pictures of vagabonds (around 50 of them), hung on the wall by the late artist Birgir Andrésson (1952–2007) as part of a work of art, as described in the last of the three letters published later on in the book. Like my grandfather, Birgir was interested in this group of outsiders, and their values informed his art. As I walked down the 78-meter-long corridor of the Reykjavík Academy where photographs of vagabonds had been lined up along the walls, I grasped for the first time in earnest the significance of these people and the emptiness that the speed of modern life tends to induce. Each photograph was displayed at more than life size, and I had the sense of being in the middle of a tale of eccentrics – one form of the 'local tale tradition' in Iceland that my father liked to study.[4] The artist later told his biographer that when the exhibit at the Reykjavík Academy was over and he started to remove the photographs of the vagabonds

'... the scholars at the Academy wept, they had become part of the community there.'[5]

The reason why I had not previously noticed their significance is that the concept of 'soft spots' has never been on the agenda of those who follow the model of the grand narrative – the big structures that govern perceptions of reality. *Soft Spots* is an attempt to capture that emotional journey in words and pictures. The book is grounded in 'Slow' principles, i.e. allowing oneself the indulgence of exploring the crumbs that have fallen from the scholarly table, where the focus has been on sharpening the outlines of scholarly knowledge.[6]

All these photographs have led me to think about my ancestors – about the past in which they existed, and about myself. The significance of the archive for me is entirely different from its meaning for my grandfather – or I suppose, at any rate, that my place in the present time prevents me from putting myself in his place and understanding what drew him to these contemporaries. My own contemporaries, like my father, have understandably been as ambivalent about the significance and value of the archive as I was. After years of consideration, *Soft Spots* emerged, based on the interplay of the images from my grandfather's collection and texts that I wrote relating to them. Cast in the autobiographical mold, this 'non-autobiography' is an attempt to understand the chain that the generations forge between past, present and future.

A well-known Icelandic publisher died recently, leaving an extensive library. His son – a writer and book-designer aged about 40 – hardly knew what to do with the books, so he wrote a book about his dilemma called *My Father's Library* (*Bókasafn föður míns*).[7] He felt little connection to the library, which was the property of another. Yet he felt that there was a link, that some part of it was, in an undefined way, his. In the end, he stepped into a world that belonged to the 'local tale tradition,' and discovered a gateway he had not even known existed. That experience is not unlike my own when I suddenly understood the true value of my grandfather's photographic archive – not only for him, but also for me. The *Archive* as a phenomenon had a story to tell which was hard to understand, for the object itself – the archive – reflected a past that I did not know existed. The *Archive* has provided the three of us – my grandfather, my father and me – with a reason to mirror ourselves in the past and in the present; and that experience forms a thread that runs through all our lives.

In this book that experiment acquires new meaning for those who examine the archive – whether our family members, or the general reader. Again, it might be considered a 'potential history,' as the Polish historian, Ewa Domanska, argues when she explores unrealized potential in the past in an attempt to show what conditions should be created in order to allow people to become accustomed to each other, and how they could coexist, even in conditions of conflict, as she puts it in an article from 2018, 'Affirmative Humanities.'[8] I will explore these concepts toward the end of the book, after the chapter on the non-autobiography, but first I will discuss the meaning of ego-documents in general for the discipline of history and their power for the individual when he or she recalls memories from the past. For that reason I will start with my own recollection of past memories, with the aid of my family memory.

In the chain that constitutes the *Archive*, every link is broken and worn out, so one must apply all one's efforts in order to establish a continuity.

An ante-mortem photograph

Ingimundur *fiddle* channeled all his energies into his art, traveling about with his violin and playing for people. For years he never let up; he carried on and performed with delight. But there would always be individuals who felt compelled to crush his sparkling spirit and demean him.

The adversity was painful, but Ingimundur carried on undaunted, until the time when he encountered a man in Reykjavík – a person who could not stand to see Ingimundur's playful joy. He simply had to quench that flame. Ingimundur understood at once that he would not recover. He decided to seize the moment before the end, and have his picture taken. He felt that he would then be prepared to meet his fate.

The man who had kicked him in the head as he lay on the ground never knew the consequences of his deed. Yet, in later years, he would boast that he had met Ingimundur *fiddle* in Reykjavík, though he would not recollect the precise events. He had a picture of him in his mind, just before he died.

Notes

1. I mention only two books here to give an idea of the steady stream of studies that turned against the grand narrative, but the list of possible studies is long: Alun Munslow, *Deconstructing History* (London: Routledge, 1997); Alun Munslow, *The Future of History* (London: Palgrave Macmillan, 2010).
2. Sigurður Gylfi Magnússon, *Snöggir blettir* (Reykjavík: Miðstöð einsögurannsókna and Ljósmyndasafn Reykjavíkur, 2004).
3. See a new article on the history of emotions soon to be published: Sigurður Gylfi Magnússon, 'At the Mercy of Emotions: Archives, Egodocuments and Microhistory.' *The Routledge History of Emotions in the Modern World*. Katie Barclay and Peter N. Stearns, eds. (London: Routledge, 2022), forthcoming.
4. The illustrations in this part of the book – Episode I – are all from the collection of the artist, Birgir Andrésson, who gave them to me in exchange for some of my grandfather's photos.
5. See a book on Birgir Andrésson written by Þröstur Helgason, *Birgir Andrésson: Í íslenskum litum* [Birgir Andrésson: In Icelandic colors] (Reykjavík: Crymogea, 2010), 119.
6. See discussions about the most important concepts of the slow ideology in the following books: *Slow Space*. Michael Bell and Sze Tsung Leong, eds. (New York: Monacelli Press, 1998); Robert Levine, *A Geography of Time. The Temporal Misadventures of a Social*

Psychologist, or How Every Culture Keeps Time Just a Little Bit Differently (New York: Basic Books, 1997). See also a website about the 'slow' idea called the 'slowlab': www.slowlab.net/. See also: Isabelle Stengers, *Another Science Is Possible. A Manifesto for Slow Science,* transl. Stephen Muecke (London: Polity, 2018).
7. Ragnar Helgi Ólafsson, *Bókasafn föður míns. Sálumessa (samtíningur).* (Reykjavík: Bjartur, 2018).
8. Ewa Domanska, 'Affirmative Humanities,' *History – Theory – Criticism*, 1 (2018), 9–26.

2 Family Matters

Memory and the Importance of Egodocuments

At the Homefront

In October 2000, my father, Magnús Helgason, died suddenly at the age of nearly 84, having been in excellent health. He was a letter-writer. In his many decades of work as managing director of commercial,

DOI: 10.4324/9781003177661-2

contracting and industrial enterprises, he had to have dealings with a huge number of clients, in Iceland and abroad – by letter. I was aware of this, and as a boy I often observed him as he wrote letters in his office. Later, when I went to the USA in 1985 to study for my doctorate at Carnegie Mellon University in Pittsburgh, I benefited from his diligent and devoted letter-writing. I replied in the same way, and for a time I wrote numerous letters to my parents and to friends and relatives. In memory I felt I had been quite an avid correspondent, and I recalled letter-writing as having an effect on me akin to psychological counseling from a professional. It gave me an opportunity to describe what I saw in my new surroundings, and to sum up what I felt was important about my experience.

My early months in the USA were like a vitamin boost for me as a scholar; and I felt I would never get enough of discussing my impressions of each passing moment. My fellow-students, who were from all over the world, were also untiring in discussing the new trends and ideas into which we were plunging – and that gave rise to a most memorable ideological phenomenon which deeply affected all who took part in it. Over days, weeks and months, we sat over ideas that found their way onto our program and embarked on endless debate on specific aspects of our engagement with the past and our discipline. Looking back, I feel that I was born into a new world, which has informed my thinking and ideas ever since. I had a lot I wanted to say, and I felt I needed to communicate it to those who wanted to hear it. My father was keenly interested in everything to do with history in general and the academic discipline – and he sincerely shared that enthusiasm with me.

As time passed, the memory of the significance of those writings grew vaguer; but shortly after my father's death, they acquired a new meaning. My mother, Katrín Sigurðardóttir, who celebrated her 100th birthday in February 2021, sold the home where they had lived for nearly forty years – which had been my childhood home. In clearing the house for the move, about 100 letters came to light, written by me to my parents, mostly in 1985–1988.

Astonished, I started to read. I felt I had the opportunity to revisit memories of my experiences at that time, to which I had given little thought in recent times. And in a sense a new view of reality was opened up to me. Reading the letters led me to search out the letters I had received during my nine years in the USA. So far as I remembered I had thrown little or nothing away, but I had not consciously preserved the letters. I went down to the basement of my home and started rummaging through boxes, revealing a large number of letters which had survived in envelopes and folders among my things.

I started reading, and sorted the letters chronologically. I rapidly realized that my father had been a prolific letter writer, and I estimated that he had written me nearly 500 letters over that period. Most survive, although some have been lost. I think it is likely that I also received some hundreds of letters from other family members and friends. Reading the letters opened up to me a period of the family's life, and events in the family history, which I had almost totally forgotten. And, what is more, many of the memories I had contrived to forget related to dramatic events in my life and the lives of people with whom I had family ties. In other words, I stood face to face with a revelation of my own life, and was astonished! My father had sent me about a letter a week, in which he reported what had been happening in his life, and that of others in the family. Reading the letters gave me an extraordinarily clear image of family history, and at the same time of my own life.

My father was in the habit of starting his Monday mornings at work by rolling a sheet of paper into his typewriter and writing about life in Reykjavík. On his way home at lunchtime to eat with my mother, who was a home-maker, he would post his letter to me, and a few days later, it would reach me on the other side of the Atlantic, in faraway Pittsburgh, Pennsylvania.

In the years between 1985 and 1994, technology transformed our means of communication. It became cheaper to pick up the telephone and call, while the fax offered new possibilities. My father, for instance, started to fax his letters to me, so I received them instantly. From the time when this new technology was introduced, he would send me brief notes or comments by fax – just as we use email and social media today – and I have not necessarily kept those. For a long time he continued to send his letters by mail, just as a back-up to the fax! I have almost all the letters, and many of them in duplicate. The fax also came in useful as I was finishing my doctoral thesis, but far away from my primary sources. My father stepped in to search out sources, and sent me copies by fax. This facilitated my work greatly, and was a huge help. I think he found it all quite enjoyable, as he went from library to library to gather material to send me. My requests for assistance were often somewhat vague, as witness his account here:

My dear son.
    As soon as I got back from Vesturströnd [the home of my brother Helgi and his family] yesterday, I started looking through my bookshelves to see what I had about the homes of Icelanders at the period you are dealing with in your thesis.

I remembered an essay on the subject in the Register of Masons and Stonemasons. I have photocopied it and I will fax it in a little while.

At the end of the essay the sources are referenced, including Guðm. Hannesson: *Húsagerð á Íslandi* [Buildings in Iceland]. I decided at once to go up to the National Library and look at that work. And to be on the safe side I looked Guðmundur up in the Medical Register, where a large number of writings by him are listed. It states that the essay is found in *Iðnsaga Íslands I* [Industrial History of Iceland] (pp. 1–300). I mention this only to show you how self-taught scholars work!

Now I'm going up to the Library to read those 300 pages and photocopy the sections I think may be useful. I point out that as I write it is 9.15, so you can see that I've got a lot done this morning![1]

In that way my father resolved many problems, and enabled me to complete my thesis at the prescribed time. In another letter written in January 1993, nearly a year before my *viva voce* examination on my thesis, he writes: 'I received your request, and I had no trouble at the National Library in getting the photocopies, which I am faxing herewith. Don't hesitate to send me more tasks, I'll be happy to resolve them.'

I should point out that this was before email was in common use; and indeed my father never managed to master that, although he learned to use computers for his writing when he was approaching eighty.

Reading my own letters, and those I had received during my time in the USA, had an unsettling effect on me. Shortly afterwards I had the opportunity to spend six months in Pittsburgh pursuing research, on a Fulbright scholarship.

As I walked about the streets and squares of the city, memories of past times came flooding back – memories I had long ago forgotten or 'put away,' but I now realized how important they were to me. I understood that they were a major aspect of my personality and reality, despite the fact that I had not consciously worked with them for many years, I felt I had a better understanding of my place as a foreigner in another country, and the impact of that on my self-expression on scholarly subjects, and also on my own personality. Because my confrontation with new circumstances, a new language and new culture was a hard one, the course of events and individual fragments of memory have given rise to reflection which has intensified my memory of that time.

Canadian scholar, Eva Hoffman, writes about this aspect of self-expression in her autobiography, *Lost in Translation*: she had found herself in the situation of having to learn her way in a new environment and a new language when she moved from Poland to Canada as a girl. That change complicated not only her ideas of self, but also her general self-expression about life. The memory of her life after emigrating from Poland was colored by bitterness, and by joy over her new situation.[2] 'In English, words have not penetrated to those layers of my psyche from which a private conversation could proceed,' writes Hoffman. She continues:

This interval before sleep used to be the time when my mind became both receptive and alert, when images and words rose up to consciousness, reiterating what had happened during the day, adding the day's experiences to those already stored there, spinning out the thread of my personal story. Now, this picture-and-word show is gone; the thread has been snapped.[3]

Hoffman's evocative description of the importance of language is particular illuminating, as she discloses the difficulties that face those who enter a new language zone and must remember and think in a new way, in a new linguistic environment.

I freely admit that my own experience was not especially dramatic, but nonetheless my situation certainly had an impact on my perception of my surroundings and the material I was learning about. In the native tongue, a concept has resonances beyond the direct meaning of the word, a significance which the native speaker learns to understand at a young age, and which enhances comprehension of more complex ideas as the years go by. In a new language environment, that grasp of concepts is weakened, because dictionaries tell only half the truth. In such circumstances the struggle with a new language becomes strenuous and wearing.

The senses are all strained to the utmost, and every effort is made to understand and grasp the context. Such feelings are clearly discernible in my letters of that time, and my memories are similarly colored by my position as a foreigner in a society of 'foreigners' – a defining feature of US society, which is avowedly multicultural. Hence, my memories bear the stamp of having been thought and received in a language in which I was initially not at home.

I realized as I walked around the city of Pittsburgh that it was of the greatest importance to nurture one's own memories, and thus to attain a certain calmness of heart, almost spiritual calm. That is far from being what a middle-aged man is thinking about in the bustle of daily life, and indeed it is hardly possible to maintain that I have succeeded in attaining a harmonious life! But, all in all, I prize the opportunity I had, and I understand and perceive its importance for my wellbeing in the future. For memories are more than moments of the past. We have put into each memory our ambitions, thoughts and values that are extraordinarily close to us – that is, if we succeed in strengthening our bonds with our past.

Nobel-prizewinning author, José Saramago, interviewed by Icelandic journalist and literary scholar, Þröstur Helgason, was asked whether it was true that he had little faith in the history that had been written: 'Iceland's past will never be written,' remarked Saramago. He went on:

> But it is possible, on the contrary, to write one, two, thirty, forty histories of Iceland. But Iceland's history is not Iceland's past. In the past is everything. But if we write the history of a country, or of a person, we cannot claim that everything in the past of the country or the person is in the history. That would be a lie. A historian selects from the past events which appear to offer some continuity, and then says: This is the history of Iceland.[4]

Like Saramago, I have maintained in my writings that the past cannot be grasped, and I have urged historians to abandon the dream of recreating a past time.[5] I have in this context rejected synthesis in history, and the 'grand narrative' which tends to impede all the historian's freedom of thought. Instead I have proposed something I call the 'Singularization of History,' which is a variant on the ideology of microhistory. The premise of this new ideology is an attempt to study exhaustively fragments that have survived from past times – not to gain an overview of history, but in order to acquire better opportunities to *think about the past*. The principal objective here is thus not more and deeper knowledge, but a more appropriate place for critical thought. In order for it to be possible to reach that place, it is of great importance to understand one's own thinking, how the *self* comes into existence, and what opportunities humans have to look back and evaluate the course of their lives. Individual memory has for that reason provided rich territory for scholarly research. In the bustle of everyday life, the human capacity to remember has declined due to endless stimuli from all sides. Hence we give up on committing to memory, constantly *testing* concepts, circumstances, the past and our own view of reality, in a new way. But in order to be able to understand the concept of testing in this way, it is vital for each individual to be able to assess the formation of their own self. The same applies to historians and their access to the idea of the self. In order to be able to address the past, it is important to study the development of self-expression on which all historical sources are based, in one way or another. For these reasons I see egodocuments as key sources for scholarly research – self-expression of any kind which offers the opportunity of putting the scholar in a position to carry out a thoroughgoing analysis of the past. This interplay of memory, memories and expression indubitably opens up unexpected opportunities for critical thought and how they relate to the historian's subjects. I have sought systematically to adopt this kind of critical thought.

I have, for instance, made incursions into various different scholarly fields, with the intention of applying egodocuments in order to demonstrate how a series of historical events can be analyzed in a different way from that offered by conventional history. I have in that process applied a critical approach to gender history, social history, transnational history, history of mentality, theory of sources, historical demography, microhistory and Icelandic historiography.[6] All these experiments had the aim of disseminating a certain ideological way of thinking into the humanities, and especially history, which has in my view acquiesced to the 'idea of synthesis' – which has been the case for most members of the Icelandic historical establishment toward the end of the 20th century and well into the 21st century. Egodocuments are here key to the ideological transfiguration which I believe characterizes my life as a scholar.

The series of events which led to my exploration of my correspondence with my relatives revealed even more. I had also kept a large number of letters I had received when as a boy I was sent to the country every summer for the long vacation. For three summers, from the age of six, I stayed at Egilsá in Skagafjörður, north Iceland, with farmer/author, Guðmundur L. Friðfinnsson, and his family. When I was a child, it was customary for Icelanders who lived in Reykjavík and other urban centers to send their children into the country for three or four months every summer. It was, of course, hard for the children to be away from their families for so long, but letters made the separation easier. I also found a number of letters from the summers I spent in Hrunamannahreppur in the south, from the age of nine and into my teens. I stayed on the farm of Miðfell with excellent people, Margrét Sigurðardóttir and her son, farmer Sigurður Gunnlaugsson. It was on that farm, nearly 80 years before, that my grandfather, Helgi Magnússon, had grown up from the age of 10 to 20 (1882–1892). He had been fostered by his aunt, Margrét Magnúsdóttir of Miðfell; she was also foster-mother to another nephew, Árni Þórarinsson, who grew up to be a pastor and became nationally renowned for his storytelling skills. The two cousins and foster-brothers, my grandfather and the Rev. Árni, were close, and my family felt a strong bond with that part of Iceland, where we had distant relatives on almost every farm. Those bonds are seen in the letters I received during those years, and it is safe to say that my relatives in that district gave me a stronger foothold in memory than would otherwise have been the case. Endless tales of the Rev. Árni and other colorful characters in the community often come to my mind. That time, at least, is firmly rooted in my memory, and has great significance in my life. Near-continuous stories recounted at the kitchen table in my home, or at family gatherings, about people from that community and relatives in that region, have stayed with me in adult life. That combination of narratives, experience and written sources has, in other words, meant that those memories have proved more lasting than much else that has happened in my life. It is almost as if I had experienced for myself how oral traditions were passed from one generation to another in past centuries, and gained a significance in the memory of those who may not have had any personal involvement. Here I experienced the collective memory of the family, working indirectly on me.

But that was not all: not only had I kept letters relating to my boyhood and my summers in the country, but also correspondence from other important times in my life. A certain continuity may be discerned in my memories; and in addition in 1996 I started to keep a diary, and have done so continuously ever since. Initially the diary was more in the nature of a book of memoranda, although it is possible to trace events in my life in the early volumes. My diaries now comprise 20,000 pages in 71 volumes; and the importance of the diary for my psyche has gradually increased. Today I use my diary to resolve debatable issues of scholarship, while also addressing personal matters more than I did when I began. What is interesting about this writing and accumulation of material is that it was not conscious. I also feel that I kept all this material purely by chance. Perhaps this explains why I have been so drawn to egodocuments in my scholarly career.[7]

Oddly enough, it has rarely occurred to me to go back and read the letters or the diary, except for some specific reason. That is evidenced by the fact that I had little idea how many of the letters I had received during my life were in existence. I never consult the diaries unless I need to look up some detail which I know is there. The writings are

all in the *now*, a self-expression which has significance at the moment of writing, but loses its importance as time passes. Even important events in my life are lost in the mists of memory, to surface by chance – just as letters turn up recounting the background to certain events, and how they were resolved. In the end, perhaps individual events have limited importance for the person who penned the words – at least an entirely different significance from the time when they occurred. This leads to my hypothesis that a human being is today – in postmodern or post-postmodern time – *not one but legion.* José Saramago considers similar ideas in the interview cited above, pointing out that the child '[...] that I was no longer exists. My body and my mind are constantly changing – I am both quite different from when I was a child, and the same person.'[8] It is thus debatable whether we can refer to an individual as being the same person all their life. In many cases, the transformations are such that it would be more appropriate to speak of *selves* than *self.*

Events → Narratives → Analysis → New Events

Those who work with narrative sources set out to address certain central issues regarding egodocuments and their use and meaning. Subjects for such investigation include how the individual is shaped by text, how scribal culture has had a formative influence on people worldwide in recent centuries and the nature of the interplay between texts (narratives) and life (reality). The basis of the scribal culture and the sway it has developed needs to be considered in an international context, with regard to the semiotic status of the text as a phenomenon. More importantly, the scholar needs to find a new and unusual path toward the formation of the sources, if they are to unfold its creation and meaning.

What is Microhistory? which I wrote with my friend and colleague, Hungarian microhistorian, István M. Szijártó, addresses a specific personal matter, where an attempt was made to understand how sources came to be, and what their significance was.[9] I stepped forward in person into the research arena as an active participant, the person who records the narrative, analyzes it and lives and moves within the events associated with it. I wished to make an attempt to adopt positions both in 'the past' and in 'the history,' so to speak – to assess my own actions in a historical text and investigate how 'the narrative' has influenced my experience of 'what happened.' In this way I made an attempt to create an opportunity to compare and analyze problems that may come up with sources from past times and address the question of how best to work with such material in academic research. I took, admittedly, an unusual approach in this matter, building on earlier experiments of mine in research on the self, when I have taken up a position within the text and used this to try to resolve academic problems.[10]

This part of my approach requires some explanation, since it will provide an unusual opportunity to analyze the interlinking of events, narratives, analysis and new events. And that was what I did in the chapter in *What is Microhistory?* where I considered four book projects that I produced, that may be viewed as 'academic happenings'! But before I give my account of this unconventional academic experiment, which I wrote about in *What is Microhistory?* I must mention that in 2009 I made a weighty application to the Icelandic Research Fund, proposing that the Fund provide a grant for my study of the place of the author in the text and how a source comes into existence, based on my own experience.

The responses of the three external reviewers were most interesting, especially when they discussed my approach as a scientist in the study. With reference to *Originality of the project*, one of the reviewers stated: 'The originality of the project is beyond doubt. The project is described by the applicant as an experiment. And so it is. Therefore, the evaluation of the scientific value of the project has to take this into account. Taken on its own conditions, the scientific value of the experiment could be high. From a more traditional viewpoint, one might have some reservations about the value of a project so closely linked to the scholar doing the project and his personal life. This is both the strength and the weakness of the project as a scholarly enterprise.' The reviewer's friendly response to the project, which (by the way) was not granted funding by the Research Fund, is illustrative of the attitude of the majority of scholars in the humanities and social sciences to such experiments, in which the author makes him/herself the subject of the study or utilizes the personal testimony of other individuals. The project for which I requested funding was this:

After many years' experience of the use of life writing or egodocuments in academic research, covering all types of historical sources as well as other related manuscripts, I wanted to explore their actual significance and meaning for scholarship in greater depth. In fact, I wanted to examine the interplay between the sources and the individuals to whom they relate, directly or indirectly. To be able to pursue the previously-mentioned approach, I became fully aware of the fact that I had to step forward in person into the research arena as an active participant, the person who records the narrative, analyzes it and lives and moves within the events associated with it. In fact, I wished to make an attempt to adopt positions both in 'the past' and in 'the history,' so to speak – to assess my own actions in a historical text and investigate how 'the narrative' has influenced my experience of 'what happened.' In this way I wanted to create an opportunity to compare and analyze problems that one generally faces with sources from past times, and address the question of how best to work with such material in academic research. I was aware, however, that it could prove very difficult to gain such an opportunity – that such circumstances would not often arise in the life of one person.

And yet, out of the blue, I found myself in the situation of sitting at every place at the table: being part of the past, and the one who studied it, wrote about its context, and experienced in real time all that the process offered. In other words, I was given the opportunity to test my own ideas, in my own personal life. This approach of mine requires some explanation, since it provided me with an unusual opportunity to analyze the interlinking of *events, narratives, analysis* and *new events*. And here is the story which I both used in my scientific application and wrote about in *What is Microhistory?*:

On Gay Pride Day (August 12) 2006 in Reykjavík, I met a woman with whom I developed a close relationship. This romance was from the very outset extremely intense, as manifested in a constant flow of letters and e-mails, text messages, long entries in my diary about the affair and the woman who occupied my thoughts, countless phone calls and hours together every day. As things worked out, before long I set about writing a book, that I published at Christmas 2006: a book project that was produced just like any other book, 166 pages, but printed in only two copies, under the title in Icelandic *Næturnar hafa augu eins og þú: Saga úr Vesturbæ* (The Nights have Eyes like You: A West Side Story).

The concept of the book was that I invented a narrator – a historian – who had acquired all the above-mentioned sources, and spun from them the tale from the beginning until December 2006, when the book was published. The fact was that the woman I had fallen for had wanted to break off our relationship soon after it began, when she realized that I was only slightly younger than her parents, and that I had a strong, though indirect, connection to her past. She was born when her mother was only 18 years old; she grew up on the same street as I in Reykjavík, and of course everyone in the street knew when the baby was born – and also knew when the young mother tragically died when her child was only six years old. I still remember the affectionate feelings I had for the little girl, who had lost her young mother. But I had not kept tabs on her later life – the age difference between us being about 17 years. In 1996, we met again, and by chance I realized who she was. We met at the History Department of the University of Iceland, where she was a student and I a teacher. But at that time our acquaintanceship was brief and distant.

Ten years passed before I met her once more, on Gay Pride Day 2006. Our relationship progressed rapidly. But when she became aware of the old connection, she was distressed, and plainly told me she wished to end the relationship. I was devastated, as I had fallen for her in record time. I wrote to her a declaration of my love. And the letter had the desired effect; after some thought and consultation with her friends, she decided to go on. But I continued to write her letters, in which I described my feelings in some detail as I experienced them. She received such epistles every two or three days, and after the tenth she remarked: 'we really ought to keep all this writing organized.' At that point I was struck with the idea of documenting the entire relationship from start to finish, with the idea of publishing it in book form in due course. And it transpired that I had a remarkable amount of written material about our relationship – the main part consisting of diary entries, naturally. I often used my diary to record my emotional state, as I passed through one whirlwind after another. Our feelings went from one extreme to another: we spanned the whole emotional scale – wept and laughed alternately, and everything in between.

In the end, the written material was all available, and the course of events was rapid and gripping. Once the decision had been made that I would write a book about us, in some form, I pursued it with passion, and worked energetically to keep records of the whole storyline in our lives – to describe the emotional roller-coaster ride of the first four months of our relationship. I wanted to convey to her, as accurately as I could, how I was really feeling. It was of course a bold notion, but a tempting prospect for one who has focused on minute analysis of events from the past with the aid of the methods of microhistory.

At a certain point, when it became clear that there was a real possibility of the book coming into existence, I started to consider the question of production. I realized that I would have to tell her that the publication was forthcoming, as she had not realized this before. I had to inform her that I must send the work to be printed, and that this meant that various strangers would see the text. As the descriptions of our love affair were very explicit and personal, I wanted her permission to continue. In brief, she approved. And, what was more, we agreed that she would compile material from e-mails between her and three close women friends about our relationship. For she had told me at the start that she would share 'everything' with them about our romantic rendezvous. I must admit that, at the time, I was far from happy with this arrangement, but had to accept it. But when I received the e-mail correspondence, (more-or-less) anonymized, the new text added a vast amount to the narrative of the book. The narrator had, in other words, plenty of material to work with; and the result was a 166-page book about the first four months of our life together!

Initially I was proud of myself for putting together this book which, if I say so myself, was remarkably coherent, and captured the attention of both its readers (my girlfriend and me). She had been expecting a few A4 pages describing how we had come together, but when she received a proper book – a printed, bound hardback with a real cover design – she was both thrilled and speechless. And I went a step further: at the same time as the book was published I had an image of a seahorse and the lady's nickname tattooed on my right leg. Both – the book and the tattoo – were obviously over-the-top declarations of my love for her. My emotions were literally boundless. I had to express my love in as extreme a fashion as I could, and those were the ways I chose. Never before had I lost control of myself in this way. And at every moment I was possessed by the whole experience. I was, naturally, living in the now – feeling her love, and specific events relating to our life together – which passed, however, at breathtaking speed. But between our lovemaking, I worked through the relationship in a text, in such diverse ways that the experience acquired manifold significance.

Though the work was intended first and foremost as an expression of my mind, an attempt to explain my deepest emotions to a woman who had come into my life, while also being a somewhat ingenuous declaration of love, I swiftly realized that what I had in my hands was something that was in many respects unusual, in that I had myself been part of a creation process in the events, narrative, analysis and then new events that occurred as our lives moved forward. It dawned on me that what had been created here was an opportunity for an innovative analysis of how a 'text' comes into being and what effect it has on the 'course of events' that the narrative is supposed to describe – and *vice versa*, how the events can come to influence the text.

Milk

A woman once told me that humans are the only creatures that con-
sume the milk of other mammals. I was perplexed, naturally enough,
as I have always been of the view that humans scarcely belong to the
animal kingdom. It could hardly be true.

Dabbi of Nes knew why the beasts of the field do not drink the milk
of other animals: dogs, wolves, giraffes, zebras, antelopes, camels,
goats, spiders and donkeys had no milkmen to serve them. Dabbi of
Nes was a milkman, and was convinced of the vital importance of his
profession.

Modern times arrived, and people stopped drinking milk. Man and
nature coalesced into one.

Through writing books, a way opens up to study the process outlined
above and orient oneself as to how important the *narrative* could be

for the individual's (my own) perception and emotional involvement in what was happening – in fact, in the whole unfolding of the relationship. Though my starting point may have been the events surrounding the way we were drawn together and what led up to it, it was in the narrative that they took on the significance that turned them into something that seemed of high importance. The experience was, that is to say, dressed up in specific clothing by the text, and this came to have by far the greatest significance within the narrative in which this significance arose. Thus: the narrative is in this sense the key to the past on its own terms. This at least is the hypothesis from which I start in my approach. It can hardly be otherwise, since the scholar's focus on and involvement in other people's texts can scarcely be other than a fragmentary and disjointed realization of what actually happened. For these reasons I believe that the scholar needs to look to ways of studying texts on their own terms, and one option here is to employ my concept of 'singularization,' possibly with the aid of the research model which I have referred to as the 'textual environment.'

The thinking behind the 'textual environment,' an approach which I have been developing systematically over a number of years, is to draw scholars' attention to both the content of the source – the textual space – and to its embracing environment – meanings and connections that constitute the textual whole. The approach extends to aspects such as vocabulary and general diction, spelling, foregrounded textual elements of various types, abridgements and the presentation of the manuscript, in addition to other factors related to both the manuscript and its creation (type of paper, writing implements, working procedures, etc.), as well as the use to which the manuscript or text can be put under different circumstances. The 'textual environment' is the totality of the space that makes the text the medium that its contents and outer form have to offer. Scholars within the field of book history have worked with similar ideas under the English term 'paratext,' denoting the various forms of books and additional material to be found in them that give a particular indication of the true meaning of their contents.[11] This concept has been applied by literary historian, Jón Karl Helgason, in his research, where he constructs a frame around the entire nexus of the text and other material relating to it, drawing on the ideas of French literary theorist, Gérard Genette, who calls this part of the 'intertextuality' of a work; i.e. 'everything that, explicitly or implicitly, forms connections between one text and others,' as Jón Karl expresses it.[12] The 'textual environment' takes account of and builds on these ideas, which go back originally to the work of Julia Kristeva. Here, however, the intention is to go further, to immerse oneself in the wider context of the work and investigate how it becomes a part of the scribal culture of any area and at different times. The approach is in fact what might be termed a sociology of texts: everything that touches the scope of any manuscript, wherever and however it enters the frame.

Obviously, this academic experiment was daring, and highly unconventional for an application for scientific funding. And indeed another reviewer of the above-mentioned application expressed the view that it was hard to recognize such source work. 'I clearly recognize the applicant's wish to pursue research in the area of microhistory beyond known and employed disciplinary boundaries. Setting such objectives is in general quite welcome. What is somewhat problematic, though, is the inaccessibility of the greater part of the material for the academic (and indeed any) community apart from the applicant. Such a limit on the employed material can be problematic for the many roles the applicant wishes to assume in the course of research.' This was quite true, of course: the book existed in only two copies, and was not intended to be read by anybody else. But the main idea of the study was this:

By approaching the material found in manuscripts through the ideology of 'the textual environment,' the scholar places the emphasis on the meaning and connections that form the whole that the text is built on and that can be identified in the totality of its environment. It is thus of central importance not to disrupt this connection between the text and its substance and environment, and to try instead to delve as deeply as possible into its background and origins and understand how the text came into being. The question that was uppermost here was first and foremost: what kinds of things can manuscripts contain? How does the text tie in with the 'reality' that it describes? And what possibilities are open to the historian to work with this material? A further matter for consideration was the question of how a text 'comes to life' in a new environment and how it can lose its force and impact under particular conditions. Is a manuscript merely the record of events that took place at some time in the past? Or can it have a wider reference in the present?

Immediately after the first book was published in 2006, I started to work on a sequel – but now with my eyes open to the multifaceted relationship between events, narrative, analysis and new events. The writing was completed in December 2007 – a year after the first book was produced – and the book came out under the Icelandic title, *Andardráttur þinn er tungumálið mitt: Ástarsaga úr Vesturbæ* (Your

Breath is My Language: A Love Story from the West Side), 309 pages. The whole book project ultimately became a trilogy with the publication of *Spánar kóngurinn: Ástarsaga* (The King of Spain: A Love Story), (Reykjavík, 2009), a work of 149 pages which, unlike its predecessors, was published for a general readership in September 2009. Here I go the whole way and describe both how the relationship has reference to the pasts of the two lovers, and how it has been shaped in a 'text' that came into existence simultaneously with the events, and moved forward in the present.

It is against the background of these three works that I have had an opportunity to investigate more closely the interrelationship between the four factors outlined above: events, narrative, analysis and new events. It is clear to me that the complexity level of each factor can increase sharply as new information enters the scheme (as, for example, with the publication of *Spánar kóngurinn*), since new events and new situations can have a major impact on the individual factors within the model. The processing itself ends in a new narrative, which again calls for a new analysis which affects events going forward into the future. This intricate and many-sided course of events has been one of the main subjects for the research I have presented here in this book. The process described above demonstrates that it is of great importance for historians to examine a source from as many different perspectives as possible, and to seek to deconstruct its meaning and position within its proper context.

The woman who seized my heart and soul as described above in the autumn of 2006 is named Tinna Laufey Ásgeirsdóttir; she is now my wife. In 2015, she celebrated her 40th birthday, and my stepson, Pétur Bjarni (then 13), and I decided to mark the occasion by making a fourth book. He made the drawings and I wrote the text of the book, which was about our life together, with the title *Kyrrlátur heimur. Örsögur og ljóð* (A Quiet World. Microstories and Poetry) (Reykjavík, 2015). The book, which is 105 pages long, was completed and presented to the 'birthday girl' at a party held to celebrate the occasion; it took her quite by surprise. We had been secretly working on it for eight months. Copies were presented to everyone at the party, and the book is also available in bookshops in Iceland. The book was the finishing touch to all the experiments with text and life – and at the same time, the desire to step forward and put down on paper material that related to me personally, and to experience for myself the feelings that many authors of egodocuments experience when their writings are made public to readers who are unknown to them.

We have moved a long way from conventional notions of the connections between events, narrative and the 'reality' that is supposed to lie within the narrative. Through the creation of the two book projects, and of the more traditional third and fourth books, ways open up to explore in depth the interplay of different aspects of manuscripts and how the 'textual environment' shapes its individual elements. Whether the biographical method, or some other, is used in that analysis, I am of the view that accurate textual analysis in the spirit of the 'singularization of history' method, which was discussed earlier in the book, will be a beneficial influence on the research of scholars in the future.

My conclusion is that one must not depart from the subject itself; that it is important to stick to the sources with which one is working, and that this is also likely to produce insights and revelations which will be important for understanding of the past. First and foremost, I urge scholars to look at the sources they have, and to do their utmost not to be drawn into the grand narrative, which will govern their interpretation of the subject. Every individual subject contains such a big story, such a complex of connections, that there is no need to look beyond the framework of the study.

Consensus

When you see this man, what do you imagine about his life? No doubt you immediately think that he must have played a major role in the progress of two European wars; that he was one of those who made nuclear power possible; that he was a member of the team that sent the first Soviet space shuttle beyond the Earth's atmosphere; that it was he who slaughtered the last of the great auks, then stuffed and mounted it. I don't know about you, but I was taught in school in the old days that all these were among the feats of Oddur the Strong from Skagi – all one continuous progression to the human mind.

Blazing the Trail – New Cultural Studies

Literary and cultural scholars have been less preoccupied than historians with the position of phenomena such autobiographies vis-à-vis the truth, and the opportunities which the source offers for recreating the past. If scholars have opted to go down that route, it is in order to explore the effect of specific ideas or concepts on the writing of egodocuments, such as autobiographies, and their position in the world of subjective (perceptual) expression. Timothy Dow Adams' book *Telling Lies in Modern American Autobiography* is worthy of mention.[13] He wants simply to acknowledge that autobiographers always lie – that anything else is inconceivable. His declaration, which is certainly striking, resolves many issues which historians have felt a need to address, while opening new and unexpected ways to the subject. It gives Adams the opportunity, for instance, to consider how it may influence a text if the author is always lying. He sets out to analyze the reasons why authors universally opt for untruth. Adams' approach is grounded in the conviction that all of life is more-or-less a confabulation – that all our writings demand a response from scholars on general communication in the present, and the position of scholarship and science at the same time: *how far can the narratives of news items in the press be extrapolated to the general application? Are they to be trusted?* asks Adams, going on to point out that '(...) modern readers have increasingly come to realize that telling the truth about oneself on paper is virtually impossible.'[14] Whether or not one regards Adams' arguments as convincing, the premise of his conclusions is such that it demands that members of the scholarly world turn their attention to a more conscious place of the individual in the world. This has entailed a reassessment of academic methods: for, if we find it hard to differentiate between true and false assertions about ourselves, the historian must surely face far greater difficulties when many different voices are involved.

British academic, Carolyn Steedman, who takes a rather different view from Adams, points out that those who make use of autobiographies must first and foremost understand the nature of the '*idea of history*' in the work, and make a comparison with phenomena such as the '*idea of childhood*'.[15] Steedman is here contrasting ideas on the different manifestations of memory – historical memory and collective memory, pointing out that these are 'constructions,' ideological constructs which the academic world has chosen to create. When the scholarly status of these constructions has been clarified, in Steedman's view, the next step is to address the paradoxes entailed by the concepts: 'History offers the fantasy that *it may be found*: that out of all the bits and pieces left behind, the past may be reconstructed, conjured before the eyes: found.'[16] Steedman takes the view that the idea of childhood is unthinkable, or at best useless. It cannot be found, because it is contingent on constant change. 'I take childhood,' she writes, 'to be a *form*: an imaginative structure that allows the individual to make exploration of the self and gives the means to relate that understanding to larger social organizations.'[17] In the first place, Steedman works with each autobiography more on the basis of memories' domain of discourse, and how a specific memory relates to the ideological systems it inhabits. Second, many literary scholars may be said to be happy to embark on experiments with autobiography *per se*, without considering whether it is likely to tell us anything about the actions and conduct of the many. The work is handled primarily as an implement: the individual's understanding of him/herself and society in text – a form of expression which is contingent upon the limitations of the language that conveys it.

US university professor, Leigh Gilmore, has thus focused on the limitations of autobiographies with respect to accounts of events which have had an impact on the author.[18] The difference between Gilmore on the one hand and many historians on the other is that the former places emphasis on demonstrating how diverse autobiographies are – that they do not necessarily comply with predetermined formulae or norms laid down by western culture. Historians often seek out those common norms, ignoring the qualities of the individual work. Gilmore writes:

So, too, what I have described as the discourses of self-representation include an astounding range of autobiographical practices which, in their diverse traditions and histories, give evidence that the West possesses no monopoly on the kinds of cultural work autobiography can perform.[19]

It is possible to maintain, like Gilmore, that the world has in recent years witnessed a *culture of confession*, which has superseded the *culture of testimony* that was dominant in the first half of the 20th century. The *culture of confession* is predominant at the present time – and may be likened to a 'wave' of narratives. People of all classes, shapes and sizes step forward to tell their stories, without any sense that they should ask permission for such self-expression. The narrative is presented on the storyteller's own terms, with no visible connection to the power cliques in society which require such texts. The culture of testimony was formed in an entirely different manner. That phenomenon sprang from a specific cultural space which was primarily based on narratives that fostered a holistic view of society, and presented the role of the individual in that process. That testimony was summoned up to strengthen the overall image – to bring out the stories of those who were, directly or indirectly, participants in some way in important events of their time. Thus Icelanders' autobiographies in the first half of the 20th century and into the latter half were pervaded by the testimony of those who had taken part in 'building' the nation – the newly free state which had thrown off the shackles of foreign rule (Iceland was a Danish dominion until 1918, and ruled by the king of Denmark until 1944). The autobiographies enumerated every 'victory,' large or small, and recounted every step along the nation's path to independence. The culture of testimony was a tool that proved useful in promoting nationalistic views, thus fostering a sense of national solidarity.

The culture of testimony is a pillar of traditional historical research that uses narrative sources. It has been used in an academic 'narrative chain' which is constructed so as to fit into the predetermined framework of society. The culture of testimony risks creating the delusion that the researcher in fact has in their hands an overview of the world which originates with someone who *knows* how the events happened. I am of the view that the majority of scholars ignores the fact that it is cast in a ready-made 'mold,' to fit into the matrix of predetermined values.

The tension in the 'narrative' which has arisen between these two opposites – on the one hand those who espouse the culture of confession, and on the other those who have used the culture of testimony to describe their lives – has led to a certain stock-taking in the academic world. Both cultures recount *sacrifice* and *pain*, which have different sources and manifestations. Sacrifice as recounted in the culture of testimony is standardized, and within the 'acceptable' limits of bourgeois life. The culture of confession, on the other hand, leads the author to *traumas* which have had a permanent impact on their life – and these are confessed. This even applies where the dramatic experiences are at odds with the acceptable norms of society. The storyteller takes a considerable risk, as his/her testimony may be emotionally disturbing to him/herself, and to thousands of others who identify with the memory. Such testimony is presented in narratives informed by the culture of confession, which has taken control and transformed all our norms in the present day. This is the soil from which discourse about horrific memories of the Holocaust, the Gulag, bullying and sexual abuse has sprung – memories which people contrived to largely erase from memory, or at least suppress, during the reign of the culture of testimony in the western world. That was the period when the world was living in a 'postwar' period following a war which had never been fought, yet had come to an end, i.e. the Cold War. It was hardly surprising that people were reluctant to come forward and express themselves about their own memories, when *time* itself was subject to laws that were hard to grasp. Life was

a 'construct' which each individual inhabited, following the example of the construction. There was no room for individual memories of a 'life' that did not exist, until the culture of confession stormed in and took control.

The ideology of diverse 'grand narratives' rose and fell during the 20th century, and the pillars of science and scholarship crumbled as the Cold War came to an end. A changed world view was crystallized in the events that culminated in the fall of the Berlin Wall in 1989, and influenced the way scholars approached the past.[20] Hence it was not only individual identity which was transformed, but also the academic world's view of its subjects. The fall of the Berlin Wall, the collapse of the political and economic system of the Soviet Union and what were then called the Iron Curtain countries, the rise of the many-headed Hydra of late capitalism after traditional capitalist values crashed and burned and the growing importance of the global market that related to impersonal processes of production – all these were events that demanded a response from the scholarly world, which seemed notably absent during the dramatic events of the late 1980s. Many scholars reached the conclusion that their 'science' was, in the end, wrong. They felt powerless in face of the above events, which took place 'on their watch.' The systems, the academic methods which had been extolled, would no longer do – whether they had been practiced at the Kremlin, in Karlsruhe or at the University of California. A major overhaul was undertaken of methods and approaches which scholars believed they had been developing and perfecting throughout the century. The outcome has been called postmodernism.[21]

Scholars called for a re-evaluation of events and phenomena which had been in the spotlight. The academic world has, for instance, seen a flood of studies that thoroughly re-examine World War II. Prominent subjects have been events such as Nazi atrocities and the Gulag in the Soviet Union, and their consequences. The Cold War – a period in history when many scholars were stooges of governments that fostered their own versions of history in order to disseminate their propaganda and legitimize it – was also re-examined in light of changed premises.[22] In this altered political climate, egodocuments suddenly became material that was worth exploring. Leigh Gilmore points out, for instance, that the emphasis on narratives of setbacks and trauma in people's lives – which increased vastly at that period – brings out certain features of autobiography, such as the importance of truth in the writer's mind, fear of confabulation and emphasis on being able to corroborate one's words – i.e. that others can confirm their truthfulness. At the same time, she states, certain provisos apply to all these aspects of the narrative of autobiographers. This is seen, naturally, in the view held by many autobiographers that they are not subject to any rules, other than the rules of language.

Here Gilmore takes quite a different path from many historians, placing emphasis on the diversity of autobiographical expression. Every story has its own qualities. For that reason Gilmore sets out to analyze specific autobiographies and pinpoint their qualities. Her focus is mainly on revelations about uncomfortable subjects in autobiographies, and how each autobiographer goes about recounting difficult experiences in their life. What makes Gilmore's perspective interesting is that she approaches the subject on the basis of the person's mode of self-expression, how they go about such expression, and what ways are feasible. She mentions two factors which must be borne in mind in such analysis: firstly, one must look for Rousseauian autobiographical confession in each text. This is seen, in some sense, in all autobiographies – in some more noticeably than others. Secondly, all narratives include fiction that is grounded in autobiographical expression. In many authors' works such a narrative mode is seen in its purest form, i.e. auto-fiction, that is the newest form of autobiographical expression. By making provision for both elements in their research, i.e. confession and fiction, interesting possibilities are established for analysis of content and conditions. In this way all texts with an autobiographical focus become valid subjects in scholarly research. The focus of this approach thus consists in the opportunities offered by autobiography to transform the historical character into narrative, rather than seeking to identify who the writer was in reality.

The act of writing autobiographical material guided by the culture of confession reflects the writer's attempt to *remove him/herself from* the overall picture. What follows is the paradox seen in attempts by many scholars in the latter half of the 20th century, to place that individual act *within* the tradition or the whole. The conflict between being part of the whole, or having the confidence to go against the flow if necessary, is one of the prevalent characteristics of autobiography at the present time, extending to all personal expression. It is essential for contemporary scholars to work consciously with these characteristics.

In the culture of confession, the individual treats historical memory as their personal experience, thus imbuing it with an entirely new dimension. Historical memory does not govern people's memories, but is a 'landmark' that one can hardly avoid seeing and judging. At the same time, the autobiographer seeks to influence historical memory by coming forward to confess to participation in the events they witnessed – however uncomfortable the consequences for their own life. The culture of testimony, on the contrary, was concerned with recognition of participation in historical memory, but without any personal claim to it, and without challenging it in any way. In this context of historical memory, a difference is discernible between autobiographies of the first half of the 20th century (the culture of testimony), and autobiographies from recent years, which have more in common with the culture of confession.

When an autobiographer decides to write their story, they are declaring that their life and conditions are in some way special, and different from those of other people. At the same time, the autobiographers may maintain that they are part of a family, a small community or a nation, and have made their contribution there.

Gilmore cites the following sentence: 'I remember, and now you do too,' illustrating the individual's keenness to make their memories public, and overstate their contribution. Through confession the self is created, because it is presented to others for scrutiny. Thus an opportunity arises to examine how an individual believes they came to be who they are, and the routes taken in that process of formation.

Susanna Egan points out in her *Mirror Talk* that an interesting tension may be discerned between the writing of biography, autobiography as a phenomenon and the reader.[23] In a sense this may all be said to merge together in discussion of this literature – biographers are in fact writing their own autobiographies, in Egon's view, referring to the famous words of literary scholar, James Olney, who long researched autobiographies and biographies.[24] Olney's declaration about autobiographers was seen as daring at the time, as it drew attention to the unclear boundary between reality and fiction. Hence autobiographies need not necessarily tell 'the whole truth,' as was generally believed. That requirement has, according to Olney's thinking, been removed from autobiography – but the tension between the author, who tells the story, and the protagonist of the story, continues to exist within the same person.

The relationship between autobiography and reader grows ever more complex in the present time; the relation is based *inter alia* on the writer seeking not only to put him/herself in his/her own footsteps in recalling the past, but also in the place of the reader. 'How much is the reader likely to believe of what I am going to tell?' the writer might be thinking. Thus the writer must be like a scholar, exploring their own experience from outside, not from within. If they chose the latter option, they would be declaring that it did not matter who believed what. 'The truth' would speak for itself. Instead the writing of an autobiography may be said to be based on a certain compromise between the writer, the teller of the story and liver of the life (the same person) and finally the reader. The self is thus hidden in the type, form and presentation of the text – and is rarely manifested openly. Egan states that for that reason an autobiography is invariably a story from two standpoints: the one where the author stands, and the other where the reader *may* stand. This 'double vision' of autobiographers is in a sense a subject addressed by many literary scholars, which opens the way to the individual for other scholars. In fact a third standpoint could be added: the one where the protagonist stands (different from that of the author, although author and protagonist are the same person). If we accept the arguments propounded earlier in this chapter, the standpoints in any text could be almost innumerable; and hence we may consider whether each individual comprises a collection of different personalities? One person cannot be one and the same all their life. With this approach it is possible to discern innumerable manifestations of the self in any text.

The crucial point is that literary scholars tend to seek to draw a distinction between the autobiographer's consciousness and the narrative technique of the work, which embraces the many 'lives' of the person. They do this by alternating between their own mentality as manifested in reality and the version of reality that is seen in the text which is their subject.[25] In this way literary scholars have identified the *creation* of autobiography, meaning both the creation of the text of which it is comprised, and also of the protagonist. In the early 20th century, scholars were preoccupied with humanity's ability to remember its past, and the reliability of such memories. In more recent years, they have turned their attention to the creation of the work, and the framework of that creation. Gradually the academic world realized that within every text was a vital foundation of fiction, which was part of the language and its composition.

As is well known, the 'Cultural Turn' and 'Linguistic Turn' in the humanities turned scholars away from their focus on 'placing' the phenomena studied in the real world, toward studying them on the terms of the narrative itself. Such studies have naturally transformed autobiography as a subject of scholarship; and I am also of the view that they have had a great impact on how autobiographies are written.

One of the consequences of such innovations in the ideology of research is that scholars have become increasingly aware of the *multivocality* of the storyteller. Contradictions and random juxtapositions of memories form part of the most successful narratives. 'Similarly, critics and theorists have,' in Susanna Egan's view, begun to insert themselves more willingly into their discussions of autobiography, first replacing critical authority with a relativist stance that acknowledges limited and particular perspective, and then often moving toward fuller participation in the autobiographical venture.[26]

In her book, Egan tries to identify this multivocality of autobiographers, and uses her findings to throw light on autobiography as a historical phenomenon.

That discourse all leads to the conclusion that autobiographies are not told in a single voice; on the contrary, they are 'mosaic' works of art based on a *dialogue* that transects times and cultures within each work – a dialogue that ends in some kind of compromise of viewpoints. Autobiography can thus be an important tool for understanding the environment and its complex significance. In the present day, this multivocality becomes all but overwhelming, as the ways to self-expression and self-construction are innumerable. Thus the 'daily autobiography' becomes a meaningful aspect of each person's life: the family video camera, the World Wide Web, photographs, medical records, chat shows on radio and TV, Twitter, Instagram and many other opportunities for self-expression make our lives a forum for constant, dynamic discourse about the self.[27] 'Where do ideas come from, and how do they influence our life?' is a question that cannot be answered – neither in an autobiography nor elsewhere. The way to the self is thus via the multivocal discourse which is part of life as a whole.

Autobiographers sometimes resort to unusual measures in order to 'find themselves.' An interesting example concerns an Icelandic woman from the Westman Islands, Kristín Snæfells, who advertised in a newspaper early in 2003 for people who had any interesting stories to tell of events during a certain period of her life. The advertisement, which was published several times, attracted notice, and Kristín was interviewed in an Icelandic weekly magazine.[28] Kristín explained that she had difficulty grasping the course of events in her own life, as she had been sexually abused as a child; and for that reason she had taken this unusual course in order to seek out information for an autobiography she planned to write. 'I'm asking people to describe what they thought of me as a child in 1956–1962,' said Kristín in the interview. 'How did I behave when they played with me? What was I like at school at the age of seven? What kind of child did I seem to be, to adults who ran into me? I'm trying to get a picture of a maimed child.'[29] Kristín goes on to say that she is '[...] absolutely not asking for memories of drinking sessions, as some people think.' (Kristín had a severe alcohol problem for many years.) She set up a website where people could send her information about her life. She also explained on the website how she intended to go about writing the autobiography – which was published later that year.[30]

Whatever approaches people choose in the future in writing their autobiographies, it is clear that the speed of modern life has altered understanding of the self, and the individual's possibilities for capturing it. Egan points out that the new conception of the self '[...] foregrounds the cultural workings of self-invention and dignifies the humble and the various modes of identification that place us within our circumstances.'[31] In these conditions, entirely new norms have emerged, which in my view have revolutionized the possibilities for a scholar to address the present as well as the past. But in order for it to be possible to exploit the potential of the new attitudes and

circumstances, scholarship must also be prepared to take a U-turn away from first principles of history and change its emphases and methods. That means *inter alia* that the conventional 'scientific methods' must make way for approaches that allow space for study of the interplay of imagination and objective reality – of the virtual reality of daily life.[32]

Short Sigga

Short Sigga was a witness, not only to the first sighting of an aircraft in Iceland, but also to the commencement of the first motorcar journey, at the beginning of the 20th century. In Sigga's context, it is even more remarkable that the same human race that launched itself into flight could also have given birth to such a brute as Sigga's father, who smashed every bone in her body – starting when she was a child, and continuing through her adult years.

Short Sigga always longed to fly like the birds of the air. But common sense taught her that she would have to remain with both feet on the ground.

A Clear Vision

A result of the changes discussed above is that that in recent times, scholars are utilizing egodocuments from various angles, and providing an opening for the multivocality of the sources to be fully appreciated. This historiographical development has meant that the methods of microhistory have been reinvigorated at the end of the 20th century and in the early 21st century. Microhistory has been assigned far greater weight, because the attitudes discussed in the last sub-section have fostered the use of methods that could elevate the world-view that egodocuments can create.[33]

The general idea of the 'singularization of history,' which I mentioned earlier, is based on the following: the model looks inward, and studies all aspects in close detail, bringing out the nuances of the events and phenomena we choose to investigate.[34] The idea is that the focus will always be fixed on the matter in hand and on that alone: one egodocument or more – the focus is always on the subject matter under investigation. The ideology consists in researching with great precision each and every fragment connected with the matter in hand for which sources exist, and in bringing up for consideration all possible means of interpretation that bear directly upon the material. The main point here is both to study with the utmost thoroughness the material directly relating to the subject – to examine every detail exhaustively – and also to strive to bring into the study the maximum of material that relates to the subject, from its immediate environment. Such efforts often open doors to unexpected connections and 'voices,' which may offer competing explanations of specific aspects of the study.

Arguably, there are in fact two ways to approach any matter: (1) work outward, looking for connections to other issues to create a larger synthesis;[35] (2) work inward, exploring every nook and cranny – leaving no stone unturned – to fill out the 'space' that the material at hand takes up. The latter way of doing research is not the most common one among historians, which explains why egodocuments are not high on their agenda. On the contrary, historians tend to be preoccupied with the larger context, sacrificing the gain that a detailed analysis might bring to their research. I argue for a more intensive analysis of the historical sources than historians have grown accustomed to – to deconstruct their context and inner being as minutely as possible. This is the reason why egodocuments have been extremely useful for this type of research in my own approach to the past.

Care is required here because the above almost reads like a call for total de-contextualization. I try to separate the need to contextualize something I am working with, from the desire to expand that contextualization into realms of the abstract – where contextualization morphs into generalization. In fact, the argument here is about generalization – and even then, this raises all kinds of questions about what kinds of generalization, etc.

The problem with this approach of mine is in many layers, so to speak: one might, for example, ask whether it is wrong to compare one piece of material with another one from the same study? One shard with another from a different historical site? From the same region ...? Where do we draw the line, and why? Or, what level of generalization will we accept about the material we study: if we identify it in some particular way, is that not a huge generalization in itself?

The point here is that there is a tangle of issues which we too readily gloss over in our study of the past – contextualization, generalization, abstraction: I wanted to be more specific in defining and demarcating what counts as the *singular*. The problem is that the key concern – for historians at least – is the leap from talking about some specific phenomena and their concrete properties and relations to talking about society in terms of abstract processes and categories. I do try to qualify these issues in many of my works – but that is hard to do when these ideas are discussed on this abstract level, as I am doing here. Thus a new dimension opens up on past societies.[36]

Again, even if the scale is reduced in the way envisioned here, one must still expect some structural orientation within the frame of reference. But this structure must always be subject to laws other than those imposed by the traditional metanarratives and, because of their scope, must be more malleable – i.e. the frames must be more limited and more easily controlled. What is proposed here is that the essential idea behind microhistory be taken literally: that scholars place the main emphasis on the small research unit, and confine themselves largely to that. In this way the opportunity arises to give the full range of voices within society a place in historical research. The singularization of history in this sense provides the researcher with a means of bringing out the contradictions that exist between the different 'discourses' of individual groups, and that is a precondition for our being able to approach ideas and points of view that in the general run of events do not come to the fore. Egodocuments of all types offer a great opportunity to deal with complicated historical matters, because of their detailed description of limited and often well-defined circumstances.

Pose

The French painter, Manet, once engaged the most famous of the Impressionists' models, his fellow-countrywoman, Victorine Meurent, to pose for the work he later called *Olympia*. The painting is crammed with symbolism and imagery, applied by Manet in the manner of the Old Masters. Every brushstroke, every touch, that went to create the work, was consciously planned.

I find it hard to place this photograph – it is so cosmopolitan, so classic. But I recognize the subject, Icelander, Gísli Brandsson, who seems to have his own symbolic language that he applies in order to convey secret messages. Symbols and images are hidden everywhere: in the eyes, the posture of hands, the footwear and all of life. Yet a pose can also be just a pose!

Hence this ideology brings into prominence the contradictions and inconsistencies in the mind of each and every individual, and heightens the paradoxes that exist within each living person and among people who live in close proximity. In order to allow the contradictions and paradoxes freedom of expression, the emphasis must always be kept squarely on the subject matter itself, and on nothing else – on the existing historical sources such as egodocuments. The key word here is *singularization*; the singularization of history is first and foremost a search for a way in which history can research its subjects in their logical and cultural context, and thus dissociate itself from the 'manmade' ideological package of the metanarratives.

The strength of the microhistorical approach is precisely that each subject addressed is discussed both with respect to known facts, and to what is not known. The latter is, in other words, no less important to the historian's research than the former. But discussion of the unknown naturally requires research methods and approaches which are quite different from those used by historians whose narrative is broad-brush: those who work with the 'grand narrative.'

The approach often used in microhistory is called 'the evidential paradigm.'[37] The premise here is that research into small units calls for minute analysis of clues and signs in the sources; that in gathering evidence and proofs this principle is applied by detecting hidden clues in the text, and deconstructing the position of the individuals involved. In such a case, proofs as such can hardly exist, as they may in a research project based on statistical analysis, for instance. But this approach can provide an indication of the way toward certain proofs and the path the case has taken. Thus the microhistorian recognizes the *direction* of the case, and seeks to follow up by analysis of clues and signs in the sources. The method is complex, and demands great attention to detail; in applying this approach, it is necessary to bring out all the unique features found in the text – however trivial they may appear at first sight – and make them the subject of the study.

But how do we go about doing this kind of research? In a methodology which I have been developing in recent years called the 'textual environment' – that I dealt with when my love story was presented earlier in the chapter – I set out to address certain central issues regarding sources such as egodocuments, and their use and meaning.[38] Subjects for investigation include how the individual is shaped by text, how scribal culture has, for example, had a formative influence on people in past times, and the nature of the interplay between texts (narratives) and life (reality).[39]

The central element of the analysis has been the manuscripts themselves, whatever type of egodocument the scholar can lay their hands on; their creation, their context within the events they describe, the opportunities they present for analysis and how they tie in with events that take place when they are used. But we may have to ask: What kind of meaning can be attributed to manuscripts or texts of any sort that express people's personal opinions? And how can we justify their use in academic research? As a fundamental working principle, I have made an attempt to consider the interplay of *events, narrative (conscious and unconscious), analysis (conscious and unconscious)* and *new events* that arise as life moves forward. This 'living' research model I call 'the textual environment,' extending to all the aspects noted above. I say 'living,' since I take into consideration events that have an impact on the form of the narrative and the analytical process during the creation of each. This research model is certainly influenced by Ginzburg's 'evidential paradigm,' where the principle is to study the most minute details of each subject matter at hand.

A similar approach is found in the work of American historian, Luise White, in her book, *Speaking with Vampires*, in which she tackles the history of peoples in Africa who in the vast majority of cases had no written sources from earlier times.[40] Here 'texts' of other kinds became a motive force in people's lives: material that directed how they thought about and interpreted the past and their history. In these works, the distinction between public sources and oral sources, between sources that are part of the man-made landscape of societies and written sources in whatever form, breaks down; all that matters is how the sources are used in the context of time and space. The rationale for this approach lies in the perception that the sources are not solely pieces of information, but phenomena that are 'alive.' They are used to explain the background to specific conditions that are always contingent on the thinking and ideas of those who speak about them. They can be used if the 'textual environment' is clear.

Let us think about this new vision of the subject, and the possibilities it offers: at its best, a diary is a powerful mirror of its age. It can reveal the constant interplay of everyday life, individuals, community and institutions in a remarkably illuminating fashion. In this context, let us take examples which exemplify the dynamic power of such sources:

The personal perspective can be found hidden in official documents, and if properly handled, it can provide vivid insight into people's lives. The main reason is that the sources are as a rule prepared with some particular objective in view, which is only marginally relevant to the historian's subject. Hence scholars and others who gain access to such sources have a remarkable opportunity to study the individual as a person: 'One night in 1980, when I was living as a student in East Berlin, I came back with a girlfriend to my room in a crumbling Wilhelmine tenement house in the borough of Prenzlauer Berg,' writes journalist and Oxford University professor, Timothy Garton Ash, in his book, *The File*:

> This was a room with a view: a view into it. Large French windows gave directly onto a balcony, and, were it not for the net curtains, people living across the street could look straight in.
>
> As we embraced on the narrow bed, Andrea suddenly pulled away, finished undressing, went over to the window and threw open the net curtains. She turned on the glaring main light and then came back to me. Had this been, say, Oxford, I might have been a little surprised about the bright light and the open curtains. But this was Berlin, so I thought no more about it.[41]

The author recalls that story as he sits for the first time holding in his hands his 'file' of secret information about himself! The file contains detailed reports on his conduct and actions when he was a student in East Germany in the late 1970s: officers of the *Staatssicherheitsdienst* secret police, known as the *Stasi,* monitored his every step. The Stasi's code name for Garton Ash was 'Romeo.' After the fall of the Berlin Wall and the disintegration of the eastern bloc behind the 'Iron Curtain,' Garton Ash, like tens of thousands more who had been under Stasi scrutiny, was granted the opportunity to see what had been written about him. He went back in the early 1990s, to make a dismaying discovery. In the 355 pages in his file, he could read the reports of Stasi officers and their informers about his own life.[42] His file was not especially large; Garton Ash mentions internationally-renowned musician, Karl Wolf Biermann, who was the object of far more intensive surveillance. His Stasi file totaled 40,000 pages. Garton Ash found out that some of his friends had been informing on him to the Stasi. It has been estimated that one in 50 adults in East Germany were spying for the Stasi at that time – an extraordinary proportion, probably without precedent in history.[43] Friends informed on friends, family members on relatives, even husbands and wives on each other! Garton Ash writes:

> The effect of reading a file can be terrible. I think of the now famous case of Vera Wollenberger, a political activist from my friend Werner Krätschell's parish in Pankow, who discovered from reading her file that her husband, Knud, had been inform-ing on her ever since they met. They would go for a walk with the children on Sunday, and on Monday Knud would pour it all out to his Stasi case officer.[44]

Vera Wollenberger generally refers to her husband as 'Knud-Donald' in the memoirs she wrote later; Donald was his Stasi codename. It probably goes without saying that the couple divorced when Vera learned the truth!

In his Stasi file, Garton Ash was able to read about his life as it had been investigated by an official body, compare that narrative with his own diary of that time, and recall a multitude of memories conjured up by his reading. So what did he decide to do?

> My plan of action, now, is to investigate their investigation of me. I shall pursue their inquiry through this file, try to track down both the informers and the officers on my case, consult other files, com-pare the Stasi record with my own memories, with the diary and notes I kept at the time, and with the political history I have since written about this period. And I shall see what I find.[45]

And that is what Garton Ash did, demonstrating how out-of-the-ordinary official documents can be used to throw light on the life of individuals and society, and to compare them with personal writings and memories. This powerful piece of writing also leads to thoughts about all the data gathered in multifarious ways about the citizens of democratic nations – which have often been used by scholars working with egodocuments in various forms – often in a most enlightening way, as the above examples show.

But Stasi documents are not necessarily required in order to approach the individual and their actions in a new and unexpected way. One might well conceive of a study that would set out to observe one person by gathering together a range of official documents and commercial data from banks and financial bodies (e.g. credit card accounts), and comparing that information with people's personal memory. That would offer the opportunity to attain an interesting picture of people in modern society – just as Garton Ash did.

Interviews have been used around the world to throw light on unusual issues, sometimes with interesting results. In this context I shall take two examples from different settings. After the horrifying sarin gas attack on the Tokyo subway in March 1995, Japanese novelist, Haruki Murakami, decided to step away from fiction in order to investigate the incident by talking to people who had been involved.[46] The attack received extensive coverage in the media in Japan and around the world. The media reported on every aspect of the event: the members of the terrorist group, those who were caught up in the event by chance, and others who were connected to it. Everybody was under scrutiny. But attention was largely focused on the attackers, who were in a sense lionized. Among the romanticized reporting of the group of outsiders who had unconditionally accepted their leader's ideology, the victims were only mentioned in passing. 'Which is why I wanted, if at all possible, to get away from any formula,' explains Murakami at the start of his book, 'to recognize that each person on the subway that morning had a face, a life, a family, hopes and fears, contradictions and dilemmas – and that all these factors had a place in the drama.'[47]

Murakami draws attention here to the importance of the interview form, and how contemporary issues may be approached from perspectives which other sources can rarely offer. His conclusion was a fervent exploration of the lives of people in a modern society who lacked the strength to resist their fate. Their lives were complex, and events such as the gas attack in Tokyo placed their existence in a new context. Murakami was able to show these people's lives in a different light from the media – with interviews that were directed systematically at them and their ideas about existence. Murakami thus shunned the media's frenzied quest for a hero, a villain and a victim – the formula which is blindly followed throughout the media.

Another example of inventive use of interviews in study of material which would be hard to approach otherwise is the work of Norbert

Lebert and his son, Stephan, who interviewed the same people – the children of prominent Nazis – at two different times.[48] In 1959, Norbert Lebert visited a group of men and women in their twenties, and talked with them *inter alia* about the burden of history and their names. Forty years later, Stephan Lebert retraced his father's steps, to explore what these people's lives had been like. The book provides the reader with an unusual perspective on 20th-century history, and also exemplifies the possibility of reaching through interviews material that would otherwise remain hidden.

The final study presented here is the one written by Phil Leask. Leask's research focuses on sources found in the Kemposki Biography Archive, truly an amazing treasure trove of egodocuments. There he found a collection of correspondence, diaries and memoirs relating to a circle of women school friends who made a pact during the Third Reich to return in 1950 to the town where they went to school. After that reunion, they continued to write to one another across the inner-German boundary, as members found themselves on both sides. Leaks also conducted a series of interviews with the surviving members of this circle in recent years. Through these sources, he managed to follow the lives of this circle of friends from the 1940s to 2016. This offers an unusual opportunity for a longitudinal social history of everyday life in the GDR (where GDR is East Germany, officially the German Democratic Republic) with insight into gender, friendship, family, politics, etc. This study is, in fact, a great testimony to the power of egodocuments and how they often open up a new and exciting window into people's everyday life.[49]

All these efforts to assess the value and place of egodocuments are worthwhile. But in the end, they will prove ineffective if scholars are unwilling to accept the validity of egodocuments as testimony about past times on their own terms. Autobiographies are subjective sources which can hardly be measured against a scale of objective truth, as many historians demand. Comparative approaches are, it is true, subject to various obvious limitations, as has been recounted here. Methods which offer an opportunity to assess whether specific autobiographies may be deemed a useful mirror of past times – or whether their subjective qualities rule them out as good scholarly sources – are grounded in an experiment which is in itself hostile to the autobiographical construct. Egodocuments are subjective sources, and their positive qualities consist mainly in the narratives formed by each writer in their writings. The methods of microhistory are connected to qualitative research, which is a very useful approach to studies where egodocuments can be used. That approach recognizes the strengths and weaknesses of these sources, and applies them appropriately.

I am of the view that in the final years of the 20th century microhistory led to egodocuments becoming sources that attracted the attention of a growing group of historians.[50] In a sense both the methods of microhistory and egodocuments benefited from the academic position that had arisen: that the subjective experience was again valued as an important barometer for the exploration of life in the past. Both were revitalized, as I have recounted above, and established themselves as crucial sources and academic tools of analysis. Hence I see Michael Mascuch, Rudolf Dekker and Arianne Baggerman as mistaken in postulating a connection between development of microhistory and egodocuments on the one hand and *'mentalités'* on the other; the history of mentalities.[51] When microhistory took off at the end of the 20th century, the history of mentalities slowly but surely died out, as I argued in an article in the *Journal of Social History* in 2006.[52] Before the demise of history of mentalities, it was hardly possibly to make a connection between these two schools, which were so very dissimilar and sprung from entirely different origins. One was an offspring of the modernist movement (mentalities), while the other was, in its new clothing, a part of the postmodern experiment (microhistory). The microhistorians' narrative is of course their own creation, but the foundation of that creation is based on the contemporary narrative found in the historical sources. The distinction

Oddur Sigurðsson.

between the past and history is thus acknowledged, but at the same time an attempt is made to gain a new insight into former times by deconstruction of historical sources to the fullest degree. When microhistorians have the courage of their convictions, to stand by their micro-approach, new opportunities open up for analysis – as has been shown and proven in the work of many microhistorians all over the world.

Notes

1. Letter from Magnús Helgason to Sigurður Gylfi Magnússon, written in Reykjavík, September 28, 1992.
2. Eva Hoffman, *Lost in Translation. A Life in a New Language* (London: Penguin Books, 1989).
3. Eva Hoffman, *Lost in Translation*, 107–108.
4. Þröstur Helgason, 'Lífið er svört skáldsaga,' Viðtal við José Saramago. ('Life is a black novel.' Interview with José Saramago) *Morgunblaðið*, September 11, 2003.
5. See the following article: Sigurður Gylfi Magnússon, '*The Singulariza-tion of History:* Social History and Microhistory within the Postmod-ern State of Knowledge,' *Journal of Social History* 36 (Spring 2003), 701–735.
6. See my discussion of the stagnant state of women's history and argu-ments for gender studies in: 'Kynjasögur á 19. og 20. öld? Hlutver-kaskipan í íslensku samfélagi,' (Modern Fairy Tales? Gender Roles in Icelandic Society). *Saga* 35 (1997), 137–177. I have criticized social history in various places, including: '*The Singularization of History*,' 701–735. The paper includes quite harsh criticism of microhistory, and the position of social history in general. See also: 'Social History as "Sites of Memory"? The Institutionalization of History: Microhis-tory and the Grand Narrative,' *Journal of Social History* Special issue 39:3 (Spring 2006), 891–913. In addition I have been critical of research into Icelandic emigration to the New World in the 19th and early 20th centuries, which I feel has fallen far behind comparable studies around the world. See 'Sársaukans land. Vesturheimsferðir og íslensk hugsun,' (Country of Pain. Emigration to Canada and the United States and the Icelandic Mind) *Burt – og meir en bæjarleið. Dagbækur og persónuleg skrif Vesturfara á síðari hluta 19. aldar.* Sýnisbók íslenskrar alþýðumenningar 5. Davíð Ólafsson and Sigurður Gylfi Magnússon, eds. (Reykjavík: Háskólaútgáfan, 2001), 9–69.
7. See my use of both egodocuments and microhistory in the following articles: 'The Love Game as Expressed in Ego-Documents: The Cul-ture of Emotions in Late Nineteenth Century Iceland,' *Journal of Social History* 50:1 (2016), 102–119; 'Views into the Fragments: An Approach from a Microhistorical Perspective,' *International Journal of Histor-ical Archaeology* 20 (2016), 182–206; 'Microhistory, Biography and Ego-Documents in Historical Writing,' *Revue d'histoire Nordique* 20 (2016), 133–153; 'Tales of the Unexpected: The "Textual Environment,

"Ego-Documents and a Nineteenth-Century Icelandic Love Story – An Approach in Microhistory,' *Cultural and Social History* 12:1 (2015), 77–94; 'Singularizing the Past: The History and Archaeology of the Small and Ordinary,' Co-author Kristján Mímisson. *Journal of Social Archaeology* 14:2 (2014), 131–156; 'Gender: A Useful Category in Analysis of Ego-Documents? Memory, historical sources and microhistory,' *Scandinavian Journal of History* 38:2 (2013), 202–222; 'Living by the Book: Form, Text, and Life Experience in Iceland,' *White Field, Black Seeds: Nordic Literacy Practices in the Long Nineteenth Century.* Matthew James Driscoll and Anna Kuismin, eds. (Helsinki: Finnish Literature Society, 2013), 53–62.

8. Þröstur Helgason, 'Lífið er svört skáldsaga.'
9. Sigurður Gylfi Magnússon and István M. Szijártó, *What is Microhistory? Theory and Practice* (London: Routledge, 2013), 141–146.
10. See for instance: Sigurður Gylfi Magnússon, *Fortíðardraumar. Sjálfsbókmenntir á Íslandi.* (Dreams of Things Past: Life Writing in Iceland). Sýnisbók íslenskrar alþýðumenningar 9 (Reykjavík: Háskólaútgáfan, 2004); Sigurður Gylfi Magnússon, *Sjálfssögur. Minni, minningar og saga.* (Metastories: Memory, Recollection, and History). Sýnisbók íslenskrar alþýðumenningar 11 (Reykjavík: Háskólaútgáfan, 2005), and *Sögustríð: Greinar og frásagnir um hugmyndafræði* (The History War: Essays and Narratives on Ideology) (Reykjavík: Miðstöð einsögurannsókna and ReykjavíkurAkademían, 2007).
11. Important contributions to research in this area include Don McKenzie, *Bibliography and the Sociology of Texts* (London: Cambridge University Press, 1986); Brian Richardson, *Print Culture in Renaissance Italy: The Editor and the Vernacular Text, 1470–1600* (Cambridge: Cambridge University Press, 1994); Peter Burke, *The Fortunes of the Courtier: The European Reception of Castiglione's Cortegiano*, Penn State Series in the History of the Book (New York: Pennsylvania State University Press, 1996).
12. Jón Karl Helgason, 'Þýðing, endurritun, ritstuldur: Ort í eyður *Fortíðardrauma*,' (Translations, re-writings, plagiarism) *Íslensk menning*, vol. II: Til heiðurs Sigurði Gylfa Magnússyni fimmtugum (Icelandic culture II. Festschrift in honor of Sigurður Gylfi Magnússon on his 50th birthday) (Reykjavík: Einsögustofnunin, 2007), 108. See also Gérard Genette, *Paratexts: Thresholds of Interpretation*, trans. Jane E. Lewin (Cambridge: Cambridge University Press, 1997).
13. Timothy Dow Adams, *Telling Lies in Modern American Autobiography* (Chapel Hill, NC: University of North Carolina Press, 1990).
14. Timothy Dow Adams, *Telling Lies*, 9.
15. Carolyn Steedman, *Past Tenses. Essays on Writing Autobiography and History* (London: Rivers Oram Press, 1992), 12.
16. Carolyn Steedman, *Past Tenses*, 12.
17. Carolyn Steedman, *Past Tenses*, 11.
18. Leigh Gilmore, *The Limits of Autobiography. Trauma and Testimony* (Ithaca: Cornell University Press, 2001).
19. Leigh Gilmore, *The Limits of Autobiography*, 2.
20. See Keith Jenkins, *Re-Thinking History* (London: Routledge, 1991), 59–70.

21. See Alun Munslow, *The Future of History* (London: Palgrave Macmillan, 2010), and Alun Munslow, *Deconstructing History* (London: Routledge, 1997).
22. See Michael S. Roth, *The Ironist's Cage: Memory, Trauma and the Construction of History* (New York: Columbia University Press, 1995).
23. Susanna Egan, *Mirror Talk. Genres of Crisis in Contemporary Autobiography* (Chapel Hill, NC: University of North Carolina Press, 1999), 1–2.
24. See James Olney, '(Auto) biography,' *Southern Review* 22 (1986), 428–441.
25. Susanna Egan, *Mirror Talk*, 2–3.
26. Susanna Egan, *Mirror Talk*, 3.
27. See discussion of this matter in the excellent *Getting a Life. Everyday Uses of Autobiography*, Sidonie Smith and Julia Watson, eds. (Minneapolis, MN: University of Minnesota Press, 1996), which includes a number of interesting essays regarding the use of the autobiographical approach in everyday life.
28. 'Gleðin var gríma. Viðtal við Kristínu Snæfells,' (My Cheerfulness was a Mask) *Séð og heyrt* 12 (March 2003).
29. 'Gleðin var gríma.'
30. An Icelandic newspaper later reported on Kristín's unconventional means of finding information, and reported on the content of the book. Kristín is quoted as saying: 'What I wanted was to get a picture of myself at that time, and to find out whether my playmates has noticed anything different about me. Children who have been subjected to sexual abuse so often exhibit a change of character.'
Fréttablaðið November 13, 2003. Kristín was applying a form of social-scientific research technique in order to gain a better understanding of her life at a vulnerable stage. The conclusion was that the other children had not noticed anything unusual.
31. Susanna Egan, *Mirror Talk*, 16.
32. For more detailed discussion of the new, challenging approaches to traditional social history at the time, see, e.g. the following: Jürgen Pieters, 'New Historicism: Postmodern Historiography between Narrativism and Heterology,' *History and Theory* 39 (February 2000), 21–38; C. Behan McCullagh, 'Bias in Historical Description, Interpretation, and Explanation,' *History and Theory* 39 (February 2000), 39–66; and Ignacio Olábarri, '"New" New History: a *Longue Durée* Structure,' *History and Theory* 34 (1995), 1–29. In 1989 the *American Historical Review* devoted an entire issue to these new challenges in history in their AHR Forum; notable contributions included David Harlan, 'Intellectual History and the Return of Literature,' *American Historical Review* 94 (June 1989), 581–609; David Hollinger, 'The Return of the Prodigal: the Persistence of Historical Knowing,' *ibid.*, 610–621; David Harlan, 'Reply to David Hollinger,' *ibid.*, 622–626; Allan Megill, 'Recounting the Past: Description, Explanation, and Narrative in Historiography,' *ibid.*, 627–653; Theodore S. Hamerow, 'The Bureaucratization of History,' *ibid.*, 654–660; Gertrude Himmelfarb, 'Some Reflections on the New History,' *ibid.*, 661–670; Lawrence W. Levine, 'The Unpredictable Past: Reflections on Recent American Historiography,' *ibid.*, 671–679;

Joan Wallach Scott, 'History in Crisis? The Others' Side of the Story,' *ibid.*, 680–692; John E. Toews, 'Perspectives on 'The Old History and the New': A Comment,' *ibid.*, 693–698.

33. A good account of this historiographical development is found in Georg G. Iggers, *Historiography in the Twentieth Century: from Scientific Objectivity to the Postmodern Challenge* (Hanover, NH: Wesleyan University Press, 1997).

34. Sigurður Gylfi Magnússon and István M. Szijártó, *What is Microhistory?* 121–123.

35. As an example of the trend toward greater synthesis in social history in the latter part of the 20th century, see Charles Tilly, *Big Structures, Large Processes, Huge Comparisons* (New York: Russell Sage Foundation, 1984). Peter N. Stearns also made calls in many of his writings at the time for more synthesis in social-historical research and attempted to show the importance of this for the discipline as a whole; see for example Peter N. Stearns, 'Social History and History: A Progress Report,' *Journal of Social History*, 19 (Winter 1985), 319–334. The question of synthesis in history generated a lively debate in the eighties and nineties. Important contributions include Thomas A. Bender, 'Wholes and Parts: the Need for Synthesis in American History,' *Journal of American History*, 73 (June 1986), 120–135. For reactions to Bender's paper, see David Thelen, Nell Irvin Painter, Richard Wightman Fox, Roy Rosenzweig and Thomas Bender, 'A Round Table: Synthesis in American History,' *Journal of American History*, 74 (June 1987), 107–130; and Eric H. Monkkonen, 'The Dangers of Synthesis,' *American Historical Review*, 91 (December 1986), 1146–1157. See also Thomas Bender, '"Venturesome and Cautious": American History in the 1990s,' *Journal of American History*, 81 (December 1994), 992–1003; and George M. Fredrickson, 'Commentary on Thomas Bender's Call for Synthesis in American History,' in *Reconstructing American Literary and Historical Studies*. Günther Lenz, Harmut Keil, and Sabine Bröck-Sallah, eds. (New York: Palgrave Macmillan, 1990), 74–81.

36. I refer here to my discussion in *Wasteland*: in the introduction I discuss a discovery I made about my subject, sometime after publication. See Sigurður Gylfi Magnússon, *Wasteland with Words. A Social History of Iceland* (London: Reaktion Books, 2010), 7–14.

37. Carlo Ginzburg, 'Clues: Roots of an Evidential Paradigm,' in Carlo Ginzburg, *Clues, Myths, and the Historical Method*. Trans. John and Anne Tedeschi (Baltimore: Johns Hopkins University Press, 1989), 96–125.

38. Sigurður Gylfi Magnússon and István M. Szijártó, *What is Microhistory?* 134–137.

39. See further discussions in: Sigurður Gylfi Magnússon, 'Tales of the Unexpected,' 77–94.

40. Louis White, *Speaking with Vampires. Rumor and History in Colonial Africa* (California: University of California Press, 2000), 3–86.

41. Timothy Garton Ash, *The File. A Personal History* (New York: Atlantic Books, 1997), 5.

42. Timothy Garton Ash, *The File*, 22.

43. Timothy Garton Ash, *The File*, 84.
44. Timothy Garton Ash, *The File*, 21.
45. Timothy Garton Ash, *The File*, 17–18.
46. Haruki Murakami, *Underground. The Tokyo Gas Attack and the Japanese Psyche*. Trans. Alfred Birnbaum and Philip Gabriel (London: Vintage, 2000).
47. Haruki Murakami, *Underground*, 6.
48. Stephan and Norbert Lebert, *My Father's Keeper. The Children of the Nazi Leaders – An Intimate History of Damage and Denial*, trans. Julian Evans (London: Back Bay Books, 2001).
49. Phil Leask, *Friendship Without Borders. Women's Stories of Power, Politics, and Everyday Life across East and West Germany* (New York: Berghahn, 2020).
50. See new theoretical discussions on microhistory in the following works from the turn of the century and up to recent times: Karl Appuhn, 'Microhistory,' in Peter N. Stearns, ed., *The Encyclopaedia of European Social History* I (New York: Charles Scribners & Sons, 2001), 105–112; James F. Brooks, Christopher R.N. DeCorse, and John Walton eds., *Small Worlds. Method, Meaning and Narrative in Microhistory* (Santa Fe: School for Advanced Research Press, 2008); Richard D. Brown, 'Microhistory and the Post-Modern Challenge,' *Journal of the Early Republic* 23:1 (2003), 1–20; Anna-Maija Castrén, Karkku Lonkila, and Matti Peltonen eds., *Between Sociology and History. Essays on Microhistory, Collective Action, and Nation-Building* (Helsinki: Suomalaisen kirjallisuuden seura, 2004); Sigurður Gylfi Magnússon, *Wasteland with Words. A Social History of Iceland* (London: Reaktion Books, 2010); Matti Peltonen, 'Clues, Margins and Monads. The Micro-Macro Link in Historical Research,' *History and Theory* 40 (2001), 347–359; István M. Szijártó, 'Four Arguments for Microhistory,' *Rethinking History* 6:2 (2002), 209–215; Binne de Haan and Kostantin Mierau, eds., *Microhistory and the Picaresque Novel. A First Exploration into Commensurable Perspectives* (London: Cambridge Scholars Publishing, 2014); Carlo Ginzburg, 'Microhistory and world history,' *The Cambridge World History*. Jerry H. Bentley, Sanjay Subrahmanyam, and Merry E. Wiesner-Hanks eds. (London: Cambridge University Press, 2015), 446–473; Brad S. Gregory, 'Is Small Beautiful? Microhistory and the Writing of Everyday Life,' Review essay in *History and Theory* 38:1(1999), 100–110; Lara Putnam, 'To Study the Fragments/Whole: Microhistory and the Atlantic World,' *Journal of Social History* 39:3 (2006), 615–630; Zoltán Boldizsár Simon 'Microhistory: In General,' *Journal of Social History* 49: 1 (2015), 237–248; Francesca Trivellato, 'Is There a Future for Italian Microhistory in the Age of Global History?' *California Italian Studies* 2:1 (2011): http://escholarship.org/uc/item/0z94n9hq; Sigurður Gylfi Magnússon, 'Far-reaching Microhistory: The Use of Microhistorical Perspective in a Globalized World,' *Rethinking History* 21:3 (2017), 312–341; Sigurður Gylfi Magnússon and Davíð Ólafsson, *Minor Knowledge and Microhistory. Manuscript Culture in the Nineteenth Century* (London: Routledge, 2017); Francesca Trivellato, 'Microhistoria/Microhistorie/Microhistory,' *French Politics, Culture and Society* 33:1 (2015), 122–134;

51. Michael Mascuch, Rudolf Dekker, Arianne Baggerman, 'Egodocuments and History,' *The Historian* 78:1 (2016), 24.
52. Sigurður Gylfi Magnússon, 'Social History as "Sites of Memory"? The Institutionalization of History: Microhistory and the Grand Narrative,' *Journal of Social History*, Special issue 39:3 (2006), 905–908.

Episode II

3 Soft Spots

A Non-Autobiography

Foreword

A picture is just a picture, is the initial reaction when the eye discerns people, places or objects in a picture plane; but later one realizes that the photograph is the truth. It looks, at least, like truth itself, a reflection of objective reality. And even later one discovers that it is far more than that.

If each picture is examined, scrutinizing the hidden worlds of symbol and image entailed by photography, the whole world is opened up. But in order to achieve that, we must pore over the photograph, allowing no light in other than our own shadow.

The method applied in this book is based upon the intention to look only at each picture on its own terms, disregarding the veracity of people or events depicted, and to express the feelings aroused by such examination. Does the photograph itself have value, when disconnected from people, events and time?

I have no interest in pigeonholing the people in the photographs, holding a 'freak show' of individuals who had for some reason found themselves marginalized in society. I prefer to identify the merits of these individuals as they appear to me – as snapshots of daily life. In order to make that possible, I strive to observe life without reference to accepted norms.

I hope you will read the following text, but that is not essential. You will certainly examine the photographs – that is almost unavoidable. Whatever you do, it will be in the context of your own thinking, which thus acquires autonomy.

Words are just words – travelling between thoughts, ideas and deeds.

DOI: 10.4324/9781003177661-3

PART ONE

November 24, 1938

My dear son!
  I thought of you, over there in Berlin, this morning when I woke. I miss you so much, and I look forward to having you home again. When I advised you to go to the Commercial College rather than the Latin School, I had in mind that you could take over the company after me, as you know. Now that you are studying abroad I find myself missing you, and I would give so much to have you here at home. I, the countryman, almost feel I might go travelling, throw off all my responsibilities and undertake a long journey. Wouldn't you be taken aback, my son, if your old man were to appear in the capital itself, Berlin, out of nowhere? Do you think I would be able to find my way in the city?
  There has been a chill in the air all day, and the men who were working on the plumbing in the Baron's cattleshed complained of the cold. Neither of them knew that a little bit of that building is mine: you see, I made the hinges on the big doors – I don't think I have ever told you that. I did my very best on that task, and I am pretty sure I did a good job. All these years I have kept an eye on the hinges. They're still there!
  It looks as if there will be a strong northerly wind this evening, lasting until after next weekend. People are going to grumble.
  No, I don't think the wandering life is for me. I think it's enough for me to look at the picture of those blessed men and women vagabonds. They ask for no mercy or pity, those poor people. The most painful disappointments of their lives were concealed, as a rule, under a shell of reserve and pride – at least in the case of the vagabonds I have known. Their journey had no end. Aren't we all on some kind of journey? I just don't know. If Helgi Magnússon were to become one of them, no doubt that would start tongues wagging. But you have nothing to fear, my dear son; I'm not going anywhere, I just travel in my imagination!
  I am awfully tired after a busy day. The scope of the business grows every day. Yet one day is much like another to me, and that will hardly change until you, my dear boy, return from exile. I will surely have a letter from you in the next few days.

I shall stop now. I am going to discuss with your mother how we can ease your return home next year. Like me, she keenly looks forward to seeing you again. We are sure, dear Magnús, that you are happy and are making good use of your time there. We are worried about you because of the situation there.

We all wish you a happy birthday.

God be with you. That is your Dad's wish.

Past Times

Love-Brandur

In 1907, the physician for the Dalir region of west Iceland sent his colleague, an official in Reykjavík, a report on the health of the people in the region. The report contained nothing remarkable, except when he turned his attention to people who had no homes: 'With respect to mentally-ill people, there have been and still are the gravest problems here. People's circumstances for caring for them are poor, and there is a lack of housing everywhere for such people, especially in cases of grave illness. For that reason mentally-ill people here have generally been confined to outhouses, and have often suffered cold in the winter and huddled for prolonged periods against the cold, and the result is that they have become contorted.' Sometimes it was necessary to 'confine such people,' as he put it. Sometimes insane people were cooped up in cattlesheds with the livestock. In some cases no-one had jurisdiction over such people, who were their own masters and mistresses.

Love-Brandur had many faces, although his contemporaries generally all saw him in the same way. He was said to be mentally ill – but in fact his list comprised simply the innumerable faces of love.

Love-Brandur died in hospital at Akranes on December 13, 1960. As his coffin was lowered into the grave, the heavens opened and rain cascaded down.

Poet and Friend

'Recently printed in Reykjavík are the *Rimes of the Settler Íngólfur* ("Ingólfur's Rimes") composed by Símon *Dalaskáld* [the Dalir poet], with his picture at the front. The interest and diligence of this man in this excellent national art, rime-versification, is admirable, and unique in our time. Símon's health is said to be good, now that he has once again been able to compose such a work. May the name of Símon *Dalaskáld* long be remembered!'

He grows drowsy, and dreams. Barefoot historians step forward, and the calm before the storm is met with the magic of the word: nothing is kept secret, and little is believed.

The friend and the poet sit side-by-side, an unbreakable bond between them. Though occasionally a new glint appears in the friend's eye and a smile touches his lips – meaningful and perhaps enigmatic. But if he were to turn his back on the poet, he would not only miss his friend, but destroy himself.

At the moment of death the friend submits entirely to the will and unconditionally declares his friendship with an open mind, saying, 'Símon is a great poet' – for he wanted to live.

Little Viggi

Look at that man. It's all right, he's used to being stared at. There he stands, upright and nattily dressed, and he looks as if he's pretty pleased with himself.

Is it possible that the first thing one thinks of when looking at Little Viggi is that he's a half-grown person, or else a fully-grown 35-year-old dwarf? Really, it makes no difference, because to judge by the photograph he himself is in absolutely no doubt about his gigantic image.

I imagine him at the bedside, and I stroke him until his head gently slips back and he goes off to sleep.

Skólavarða Hilltop

A church, an art museum and a school – yes, schools and a gallery – all neatly arranged around Alexander Stirling Calder's statue of Leifur Eiríksson – Leif the Lucky. The gaps among the buildings on the hilltop are filled in by houses and apartments.

Before the Lucky days, men used to sit here who knew there was no luck for them. They had been informed that luck had to be sought out, or built; and that was what the rock was for: hewn stones.

At the northwest side of the hill, adjacent to the jailhouse, the Reykjavík Reformatory, lived Bensi of Rein. He may well have attained some kind of reformation from the heavy labor he performed all his life, but he never came across any luck. Yet he sat all day and all year, hewing rock to build tomorrow's luck.

Then he met an old man with a cane, and at the same moment looked into the photographer's aperture.

A moment, an age, an eternity – of which Bensi of Rein is part.

Such luck!

Déjà-vu

Dabbi of Nes was no déjà-vu man. Everything he tried vanished into the subconscious, never to return. He simply lived his life, played his tricks and never thought of the past.

Dabbi of Nes was surrounded by déjà-vu people. The past was constantly being recalled, or it was endlessly demanding to be remembered. The community was grounded in such repeated memories, and it is hard to imagine a person who could not take part in such memory-making. He was all alone. He had dimensions that others could not recognize, and resolved the problems of the day with one prolonged howl. He shut his eyes and collapsed in freefall into a nook of his soul.

Then came a new day.

European Bourgeoisie

Porcelain, hand-embroidered handkerchiefs, maids who dry their eyes on a corner of their apron – and *Weltschmerz* in the democratic spirit has risen up; the members of the household put on the expression of those who have unlimited patience.

On the threshold stands Þórarinn of Melur, asking after his daughter. She had married into the Danish bourgeoisie, and in that place there was no space for a man like Þórarinn of Melur. He had been making blood-sausage, and wanted to bring a few to his daughter.

When he enquires of the maid where his daughter is to be found, she looks away. Þórarinn of Melur is informed that the mistress is *incommunicado*.

Þórarinn has always been able to speak to himself, a sort of mono-loguist, and he ambles unhurriedly over the hill and home. He smiles to himself when he has decided what will be on the stove tonight.

Business

In the old days, Norwegian Óli lived on Laugavegur in Reykjavík, and sold lime in autumn. He always traveled on foot, but never failed to admire people's vehicles. It is fair to say that he was a fan of machinery of all kinds.

In the photograph, he is seen reassuring his anxious customers. Norwegian Óli had run out of lime, but the customers needed it to cleanse the membranes for the blood- and liver-sausage they were going to make.

These were people who made blood- and liver-sausage on an ambitious scale before turning to other winter preparations for the household: making clothes, needlework and cleaning certainly took time, not to mention parenting responsibilities.

They agreed with Norwegian Óli that he would deliver the lime as soon as it arrived. In such cases, he used to heave the burden up onto his back and run into town with it. The deal was done, and the customers went down to Hotel Borg for a little relaxation before the trials of winter. And Norwegian Óli turned his attention to other impatient customers.

Oddur fornmaður, og Chr. konungur 1930

King of the Plains

The man on the left of the picture, wearing a crown, is not a king, but the skipper of an Icelandic fishing boat. This is Oddur the Strong from Skagi. The man wearing the policeman's cap with such dignity is King Christian X of Denmark, Iceland, the Faroes and Greenland. It is 1930, and the plains at Þingvellir are covered with white tents. There is excitement in the air, for the millennium of the foundation of the national assembly, the Alþingi, in 930 AD is to be celebrated. The Vikings are represented, as are European monarchies – and both categories are past their best.

'I wonder who will brandish the scepter the next time celebrations are held at Þingvellir,' muses Oddur the Strong aloud, with a thoughtful expression. 'It certainly won't be any of my family,' replies King Christian X jovially.

Rat-Petersen

Is it the madness or the beast that captivates you more? Or perhaps it is the revulsion entailed by both? History tells us that the rat and the mad one stuck together. They were kept on the ship of fools through the centuries.

In 1946, radical action was taken to exterminate rats in Reykjavík. They vanished, mostly. The same applies to the mad. Probably they went underground like the rats – or has modern science attained such perfection that everybody thinks the same, behaves the same, expresses themselves the same – just as is required of them; or is life just one mass derangement?

Rat-Petersen was one of those people who appear to have found their place in life, and do their job well. But then the year 1946 came along.

Show

The audience take their places, and there is anticipation in the air. Bicycles are lined up along a wall. Some people lean against them, waiting for something to happen.

A professional steps forward to perform his tricks. He wears a flower in his buttonhole, and knickerbockers to highlight his fancy footwork. He stands on one leg, stretches his right arm forward, and holds out his left arm for balance. Suddenly he looks like a tulip about to flower. He remains in that posture until his petals fall.

The performer recovers his composure, takes a deep breath, and gathers his wits.

Ahead lies another show in a new theatre of the streets, where his reward is the smiles of the audience who were lucky enough to be in the right place at the right time, all thinking: 'Hocus Pocus, Abracadabra – should I have a go?'

My Family, My Youth

Relative

My great-great-uncle, Eyjólfur Pálsson, began life on a little farm to the east of the mountains early in the second half of the 19th century. In time he became a smallholder in the same district, but in due course he decided to leave the land and move to the capital. He was employed as a dock worker, but suffered a stroke at his work. But he had many more years to live, and from that time he worked as a newspaper-seller on Bankastræti and Lækjartorg in downtown Reykjavík, where this photograph of him was taken. He gave my mother a fine cut-glass bowl when my elder brother was born. As a child I often stood in the parlor at home and gazed at that gorgeous object cleave the sunrays into innumerable flashes.

Speed

My grandmother, Eyríður, suffered from a thyroid complaint for decades, and had to move slowly in all her daily activities. I observed her in my youth, as she felt her way from one piece of furniture to the next in her home, as if she were about to lose her balance. There was some soothing peacefulness about all her gestures that had an impact on my mental life. The big grandfather clock which stood in the parlor awoke me to life, and the sound of it striking emphasized in my mind the eternality of my grandmother. I felt she was like the Great Wall of China, immutable.

Then Grandmother Eyríður died, and speed acquired a new significance in my life.

Óli Maggadon

I often heard the name of Óli Maggadon in my youth, generally spo-
ken with an overtone of pity, and a smile. I had no idea what the man
looked like until I found this picture in my grandfather's collection of
odd characters.

   I had realized that Óli Maggadon must have been an oddity, but I
had not expected him to look so ordinary. The picture shows a pretty
typical Icelandic male, who could have been on his way home after the
open-air festival held each summer in the Westman Islands, having
taken part in mass singing, a fair amount of alcohol consumption,
dissipation and sleeping in a cold, wet tent. His expression shows that
he has no regrets. He hooked up with a woman for the first time in his
life – although he can hardly recall how they got their clothes off and
did the deed. As soon as the photographer had taken the picture, Óli
Maggadon raised both arms in the air and exclaimed: 'It was such a
blast!'

Jón söðli

Benjamin Franklin

Long ago I was traveling with my family in the inland reaches of Árnes county when we met an elderly man who had never been outside the district of his birth. But he said that Benjamin Franklin had been a big influence on him. He had read his biography at a young age, and it had changed his life. That was what he told my parents, apparently just to say something.

Didn't Benjamin Franklin come from another district than Jón *Saddle*?

Watching

When I spent my childhood summers on a farm in the Hreppar district, I realized that Hreppar people knew how to watch. But I never knew what they were looking at. The farmer I stayed with generally spent several hours a day gazing out at what appeared to me to be an empty plain. I copied him, but soon grew bored with the tedium, even restless. But I made myself stick to it, and in the end I started to dream of livestock at night – exhausted from the day's staring – animals roving the empty plains in front of the farmhouse.

Materials

I once knew a carpenter who was good at finding materials. In every nook and cranny, out and about and along the beaten path, he would come across materials that no-one cared to claim. He would pick up a scrap of wood he had spotted, examine it closely, and frown gravely. Then he made a disparaging sound which is hard to imitate or describe, but resembled the gasp of astonishment sometimes heard when someone is taken by surprise. All the space he had at his disposal was crammed full of timber and scraps of wood of different sizes.

I was convinced he would be left in peace with his bits of wood, as nobody would care to sneak away with them to their own plot.

Joy

Rolling a dustbin down the slope of Bankastræti, in the center of Reykjavík, was a popular pursuit on New Year's Eve in the olden days. I have childhood memories from my grandparents' home of such events – or perhaps I was just told about them when I was older? But it seems to me that I watched from the living-room window as these events took place in Bankastræti. Our whole family looked on as fully-grown men sprinted away from the flaming bins. They seemed to be enjoying themselves, but my family were not impressed. I was semi-comatose at the time from indulgence in sweets, being very young, so I have no clear memory of what I thought of it.

Later I often heard my relatives talk about these events, sometimes disapprovingly. Their accounts had a strange effect upon me, and before long I became uncomfortably aware that I had an overwhelming interest in these people's behavior. I started to imagine myself in the footsteps of those who were running down Bankastræti, and I always found New Year's Eve a challenge, especially in my teens.

Upright

In a family party in a big house in Reykjavík, all the men measured their height from head to foot. This was many decades ago, and the nation was growing. To stand upright was paramount.

There was a policeman in the family, and everyone knew that a man must be at least 1.80 meters tall to be in the police. So the initial presumption was that the police officer would be the tallest. But it transpired that a sixteen-year-old youngster in the family was one centimeter taller than the policeman, or precisely 1.84 meters. The result was generally well received, the young man being a promising lad and dear to the whole family. But his cousin the policeman did not speak to him for many years after that day, and according to family lore that centimeter sent him across the seas to the New World.

In America their ways are different, and their police officers are of all shapes and sizes. The only requirement is to stand upright. And cousin Magnús most certainly did so – for he remembered that every centimeter mattered, after all.

Jóhann K. Petursson, Island.

Fatigue

I sit one evening in a deep chair, exhausted. Half-asleep in front of the TV I see Jóhann K. Pétursson, known as 'the Giant,' on the screen. Initially I am not greatly interested, but then the man grasps my attention.

Jóhann the Giant explains in the show that he has been tired all his life. Long before he made that declaration I was in some emotional turmoil; the fatigue had vanished from my body and every nerve was tingling.

I've been tired all my life, said Jóhann the Giant, and I could hardly restrain myself. Since then I have never felt weary, and Jóhann the Giant has never left my mind. It is, admittedly, a little tiring to have a giant on my mind.

Brother

I sometimes considered, as I read *Chapters of my Story* by poet, Matthías Jochumsson, what it would be like to be his relative, his brother for instance; I found it hard to imagine. The strange thing is that I was never in any doubt about what it would be like to be Kjarval's brother, when I looked at his paintings. I simply visualized it quite clearly. Matthías filled up all the space in my mind. The idea of Kjarval was unlimited.

There was a radiance about Ingimundur *fiddle* Sveinsson, Kjarval's brother. He glowed with playfulness. But the same was not true of Einar Jochumsson, Matthías' brother. He was always overshadowed by his brother, and that was noticeable. And that is hardly surprising, as he appeared to me in a text, while Ingimundur *fiddle* materialized in a painting.

I have a feeling that this difference is evident in the photograph of the two brothers' brothers. One shines, the other is shadowy.

Pennsylvania

Call of the Wild

In American society, there was a perception that in millions of people's minds resided a 'wilderness spirit.' Such people took the view that
beyond the mountains lay a better way of life, and new opportunities
at every step. Whole families moved, to start over in a new place, on
virgin land, slightly farther into the wilderness.

Travelers could be sure of coming across odd faces that had a long
and colorful story to tell – hunger, cold, harsh nature, herds of beasts
and humans – some more confidence-inspiring than others – all factors which had made their mark on these questing people.

Björn 'Mouse-Eye' was just an Eyjafjörður man, from the north of
Iceland, and that was how nature made him, but in his face one may
read the same runes that crisscross the faces of those who were possessed by the Wilderness Spirit. Yet he never ventured far, hardly leaving his home district – at most he went into the mountains. The call
of the wild!

A Place in the Landscape

The Grand Canyon in Arizona stands in the landscape with extraordinary weight. It is almost impossible to imagine it existing anywhere else on earth. For thousands of years it has gazed up into the blue sky, and time has passed.

Mangi of Árbær had the same place in life for as long as he lived. His role was to be a farmhand on a farm outside Reykjavík. Mangi would occasionally go into town, meeting people here and there along the way.

Mangi of Árbær had the same landmarks in his landscape all his life, and as a rule he knew where he would lay his head that night – just like the Grand Canyon.

Social Disability

Freyjufár is a remarkable word, and not really 'politically correct.' The word was coined by Dr. Steingrímur Matthíasson as an Icelandic name for what used to be called 'venereal' diseases (today sexually-transmitted infections). Substituting the Norse goddess, Freyja, for the Roman Venus, the source of infection is identified as Icelandic – only she would do, according to the experts. Dr. Steingrímur had a poetic streak – not surprisingly, since he was the son of poet, Matthías Jochumsson.

Brynki of Hólmur was always a bearer of good news. He could, admittedly, be rather crude and cantankerous, but he was a real man.

Celebration

On November 9, 1989, my heart was filled with overwhelming delight. I rejoiced so ardently that I was confined to bed for days. In retrospect I don't know what I was thinking; maybe that day was just a good one for venting such feelings.

Jón *Mustard* was long dead by that time, yet nonetheless he rejoiced until the very end of his life. He needed no special occasion, nor did he need to be part of some great loss, in order to paint the town red: he simply celebrated continuously, without looking back. Jón *Mustard* had constructed a wall around himself, which shielded him in his celebrations.

Endless, eternal celebration within the walls.

PTL

Praise the Lord! exclaimed Tammy Faye, echoed by her husband, Jim Bakker. They established the renowned PTL Ministry, financed by contributions from American senior citizens, all for the glory of God.

Howard Stoertz, Jr., a street sweeper in Philadelphia, shared with Bogga, the bread saleswoman in Iceland, a belief in God. When he came home after a day of hard labor, he turned on the TV and heard Jim and Tammy Faye Bakker preach the gospel. They were full of energy and cheer that easily percolated into the consciousness and spirit of Howard Stoertz, Jr. They maintained that it was vital to pursue ambitious plans for the development of a church and congregation they named Heritage USA – a Christian theme park, if you like. And Howard Stoertz, Jr. and others like him were keen to contribute. Jim and Tammy Faye were his friends, and he knew that by supporting this cause he was doing God's will.

Nobody knows how Bogga, the bread saleswoman, managed to do her God's will, before the days of PTL and TV. And what happened to all God's children left behind when the corruption in Heritage USA was exposed? Jim in jail, and Tammy Faye always in tears – until she wept her way into a new marriage.

Shadow

Curved, clean, clear lines that form a shape that changes as the light alters – that is a shadow. Its movement is mercurial, and the relationship with the original is sometimes ambiguous. The shadow is two-dimensional, the original three-dimensional.

Big deal, was said to me as I stood by a house wall half-naked in the scorching heat in western Pennsylvania, maintaining that my life expectancy was greater than that of others because I had such a long shadow.

Big deal was really all one could say in the circumstances.

The outlines of Haukur, the clothes-presser, are clear, like a shadow. His three-dimensional appearance is also evident. An examination of his face reveals a new dimension on which no shadow falls – it is in a silent vacuum, and requires no nourishment from light or changing light conditions.

Big deal!

PART TWO

November 24, 1993

My dear son

I'm sitting here in my office on my birthday, looking out over the mirror-smooth bay. This autumn has been unusually fine, and eventful for us, your parents. But at the front of my mind is your big day, 12 December next. This has been such a long process that one almost forgets when it was that you set off out into the world. Your mother and I hope that you will come home for good next year, for this is your home. Our country must be a fixed place in your existence – otherwise you will simply lose your footing in the mass of nations. I'm not going to preach at you. You must make your own decisions. But your works are, fortunately, on Icelandic popular culture. We keep our hopes up.

In your last letter you asked me to send you the photographs of vagabonds that your grandfather collected, which I gave to you some years ago. It has not proved easy to find them among your things, but they are sure to turn up. Are you planning to use them for your thesis, or are the old roots taking hold of your heart? Your grandfather would be astonished and delighted, if you were able to use those pictures in America. His delight in those poor unfortunates was extraordinary. Most of them had fallen victim to liquor, or else simply to ill health. But there was something else your grandfather saw in them, that I never understood. They are all gone now – wherever they went. But I do enjoy your interest in the local tale tradition.

Won't you certainly be coming home in the spring? The company is doing outstandingly well, especially after your brother Helgi took over. It's good to stand side-by-side with him.

With love from your Dad,
Magnús.

Back Home

Workhorse

For many years, a laden packhorse had stood in one place near the Elliðaár river; one had no idea where it was coming from, or where it was going. The only thing we knew was that it was close to the old horse trail out of Reykjavík. And it seemed to be headed in the direction of the road across the mountains, but it was hard to say.

After all, the horse just stood there.

You sometimes hear about recalcitrant horses simply standing and refusing to move. My understanding of that idea was much informed by the horse standing by the Elliðaár river.

Until one day the horse came to life after many years standing in one place, and I realized it was a statue.

The mare had foaled, finally. For decades the City of Reykjavík had deemed it too expensive to have the foal cast in bronze to follow its dam.

The little foal brought the beast back to life, and I started once again to think about how two can be company.

Two Friends

In one man resides the primal force of humanity which can be exerted for good or ill. Two men pose a threat arising from the potential offered by their power.

In the Bosnian war, young middle-class men went in twos to rape women of other ethnic groups. The women who were not killed after relentless torture and rape were passed from gang to gang as sex slaves.

Gvendur, the fishmonger, and his friend, Ásmundur, probably never heard of Bosnia in their day – as they lived in the first half of the 20th century, when other people, and representatives of quite other nations, were doing the killing.

But what if Bosnia had been on the other side of the mountains in their time, and what if Reykjavík people had invaded it?

Uphill

Those who climbed Everest in their time remarked that the ascent of the mountain had been arduous. I immediately felt that it could not be so. These men had never found anything strenuous.

Gunna of Hjálmsstaðir never climbed Everest, having no reason to head for the peak. But her entire life was an uphill struggle. Her camping gear was simple, neither wind- nor waterproof. Although she might occasionally take pride in reaching a high point, she never looked out over land and continents, nor did she address her nation in a live broadcast from her destination.

The women who are hurrying out of the picture, headed in quite a different direction from Gunna, later told their story, frankly and fully. It transpired that their lives had been an uphill struggle and that their mountain ranges had all been in the lowlands – just like those of the many others who had to scuttle out of the picture.

Painting

I sometimes come across people who seem to me to have stepped out of a painting. But I never meet anybody I feel belongs in a novel. I have no explanation for that feeling, but I suppose that my perceptions are simply like that. I have heard, for instance, of people who see the whole language in colors. Every word has its color, and conversation looks like a manifold rainbow in their minds.

Measurements

38×44×44, and my muscles clench for comparison with strongman Gunnar Salómonsson. The day's tasks demand effort. Gunnar appears to have built up his strength because he felt the need to fight against being overcome by the multitude. No doubt he thought like Nietzsche, who took the view that many people felt lonely and afraid if they went against the flow. But didn't Gunnar simply want to be his own man – and didn't he, like others, regard no price as too high for that privilege?

Is it not fear, indeed, that we sense in Gunnar Salómonsson's intense gaze – a fear that he can neither overcome nor put into words? It seems to me that he is struggling to form the words that are caught in his vocal chords, and clenches his fist just to gain the power of speech.

The measurements are simply meant to distract our attention from the nub of the matter: the trials entailed by human experience.

Campaign

Liquor, a barrel and a head – and the photograph was taken long before the selfie stick was invented.

Isn't that all one needs to be drunk – or empty-headed?

Capital

Sale! Sale! – Sæfinnur with Sixteen Shoes – all on sale!

'Why has no-one come up with the idea before, of naming a shoe shop after the legendary eccentric of that name?' I asked myself. And what do you know: before long a similar advertisement was soon heard from a secondhand bookshop that had been named after the wandering chanteur, Gvendur *dúllari*. Naturally enough, sellers of secondhand books base their business on cultural capital.

– A word or two, and your fortune is made.

Stutti Bjarni

September Day

Buildings have meaning. The taller they are, the more exalted the meaning. Buildings are attributes of the day, signifiers of limitless ideals.

Short Bjarni's center of gravity was low down in his body. He could not easily be shifted. He generally waddled across tussocky territory, bare of all buildings or other traces of human presence.

Into Another Mind

Gísli. þingm. Bolvíkinga

Question and Answer Session with a
Representative of the People

QUESTION: What is your attitude to nature?

REPRESENTATIVE of the PEOPLE: Nature... nature, I know where to find
it. No, no, to hell with it. If people can't provide for themselves in
autumn, they'll have to die wherever they happen to be. That is
nature.

QUESTION: Are you opposed to industrial developments?

REPRESENTATIVE of the PEOPLE: Now, my good man, you are alluding
to the attitude of the people I represent, the people of the country.
Let me explain their attitude: Jón of Brekka, for instance, has on
his right hand a little finger and ring finger which are of equal
length and fused together, both with nails. He has no other fingers
on that hand, except for a lump of flesh low down at the edge of
his hand, level with the middle of the palm, which is just about
three inches in length and as thick as the wrist of a six-year-old

child, though tapering outwards. On his left hand Jón of Brekka has a thumb – which is, however, longer than most men's thumbs, and curves at the end towards the crook of the hand. Instead of a little finger he has a small stump, without joints, but similar in thickness to those of other men. He has no other fingers. All the siblings are also without toes, as well as being fingerless. – Heavy industry, did you say? Wasn't that what you were asking about, my good man? Of course we want more heavy industries – that is all progressive, but certain sacrifices are required. Well, sacrifice or not. Heavy industry is the watchword.

Thought

The thought that I feel has been most exhausting is when I have found myself thinking of the immeasurable space in which this uncountable mass of heavenly bodies floats – each planetary system bigger than the last. This is, of course, beyond my understanding, yet I feel I cannot help but ask myself: How can Space, that huge space, large though it may be, be limitless? Yet I feel that there can be no limits. When I start to consider the arguments for that, I find it much easier to demonstrate that the Universal Space is without limits – yes, that it can have no end.

Poet Tómas Guðmundsson Describes a Man

It would probably be absurd to suggest that Ingimundur belonged to any specific ideology or movement. He had no education which would lead to his being identified with proper music; and while his lack of accomplishment leads one to think of today's pop music, he really had nothing in common with it. He had far too much to say for that to be the case, despite all his charlatanism, which is most clearly manifested in his advertisements and programs. These are a hotchpotch of Bach, Beethoven, Mozart and Mendelssohn, alongside ditties about snipes, golden plovers and whimbrels, and all that. 'I play the violin, with variations, for my esteemed audience,' he says. No less remarkably, 'he plays some tunes on a single string, from start to finish,' and even with the instrument 'on his head and on his back, for he is a virtuoso.' And Ingimundur knows his people. They find him hilarious, having no idea that this is nothing but a pathetic mask which he dons, consciously, on his constant wanderings as he flees from one humiliation to the next. No one will ever enquire about the feelings concealed beneath that exterior, and there is no hope that his 'concerts' will ever attract anyone other than drunken youngsters and hooligans. ... This is the sad fate of this martyr to his own artistic tendencies, who by his nature was a man of rare sincerity and purity of heart.

Óli prammi

Health

My experience, and that of pedagogues in general, is that children who are born physically healthy, as I was, do not generally inherit lifelong fear. Such a condition is a function of the way the child is raised. I have suffered mentally almost all my life. I have suffered from fear, self-blame, yearning for the past, desire for love, and feelings of loss. From the age of forty-four until I was forty-eight – a continuous period of four years – I was possessed by utter despair because this love of mine – pure, healthy, solid – was horribly abused. I was robbed, tortured and in agony. I have *never* lost my mind in the absolute sense. Instead it is like this; I have *not* had control of my feelings, for my soul's structure is of such a nature that I am *susceptible* and *emotionally sensitive*.

List of Assets

Clothing

3 undershirts, one of them new.

3 underpants, all archaic.

2 outer trousers, one newish, the other ancient.

2 between-shirts. One of old homespun cloth, the other of linen, newish.

1 jerkin, newish

1 undershirt and robe, new, of homespun cloth and another old one.

2 waistcoats, newish, one of worsted, the other of homespun cloth, and a third tattered garment, almost ruined.

1 scarf, newish.

2 hats, one new, the other rather worn.

2 under-socks, new, below 2 half-socks, both archaic.

2 neckerchiefs, one new, the other almost ruined.

2 smocks, one new, the other rather worn. For a bed, one pillow and a headrest with new outer covers.

Aviation

Just now I saw from my window something that has never been seen in Iceland before – and 20—25 years ago, and even more recently, few people ever imagined happening for mankind, let alone here: there were men flying in the air. I did not see any man, admittedly – only the wings and the machine itself that propelled them forward – and so nimbly, with all sorts of swaying and graceful swings as when a bird on the wing is at play in the air.

Eyjólfur ljóstollur

Thirst for Life

But whether it is alcohol or water or milk or tea, or temperance, I thirst for, I do not know. But were I offered a drink in these thirsty times, I'd drink it, whether it was called 'life' or 'death.' This thirst is probably a family trait. I have heard that my grandmother was once so thirsty that, when she had tried all other drinks, she closed herself up in the barn loft for three days and drank firewater, but that didn't burn up her thirst so she could stop there, and then she went and thrashed and beat one of her daughters – but with the comment that she did it only to cool herself down, so the girl should not take it personally. That did little to slake her thirst, and she tried to cool herself down with tears, then lovemaking, then coffee, then headaches and finally it was exhaustion which took pity on her and allowed her to rest. That was followed by emptiness and silence, then peace, then light, then religion, then contentment, then death, then life, and that was the last I heard of her.

There have been few days in my life I have enjoyed more than the day of her burial.

Different Times

Soapbox Orator

I see myself standing in front of the Soapbox Orator with jittering nerves in Austurstræti in downtown Reykjavík, in the afternoon, in poet, Dagur Sigurðarson's *Two Icelands*. And the woman in the clock steps out onto Lækjartorg Square, walks straight over to me and asks the time.

'We live in a time when old age is revered,' I reply, glancing at the clock. 'In the Golden Age of security, and I am paralyzed with fear.'

All I can do is wait and listen and the time is twenty-five past two.

Condensed Word of God

Words are bought and sold – power and words go together, if well managed. But so much more is needed for reality to be made plain. That requires belief, conviction and above all soft spots.

Sigurður Sigvaldason had these attributes in abundance. He used them every day on Lækjartorg Square for decades. Sigurður had given thought to the relationship between power and words, and felt he understood what was required in order to apply them correctly, in the interests of the cause he believed in. He had condensed that understanding into two sentences which he called out endlessly over the square: 'Condensed word of God. Jesus Christ in calfskin for one *króna.*'

Jón Sinnep

Balancing Act

On the plain the human being finally stretched out and ambled unhurriedly along the time-scale. It was a huge effort, to manage to stand upright and look down at one's toes without losing one's balance. You couldn't call it progress. But the talent was an addition to the diversity of life.

A bottle stands on a tripod table, and there is restlessness in the air.

Metamorphosis?

PAST: Limp on one limb.
PRESENT: One stroke of the foot and the whole engine is lubricated.
PAST: Símon *Dalaskáld.*
PRESENT: Björk.

Chain

The watchmaker sits all day at his work, putting something of himself into the objects he makes. He is reluctant to sell the products, for it gives him the feeling that his heart is being torn out.

Cheerfully, the customer leaves the watchmaker's premises. The fine timepiece goes into the vest-pocket of the new owner, where it ticks in time with the heart, until it stops.

At the eleventh hour, it is decided that the watch is not to be buried with its owner, but handed down to the next generation. Everyone appreciates its beauty and fine craftsmanship. The relative, who is young, is enormously proud of the prized possession, feeling that he has acquired a share in the time of the deceased.

Regardless of changing fashions, and garments that were no longer suitable for such an object, he decided to handle the watch every day, and he adapted his clothing to it, to the delight of all. The beauty of the thing was in no way diminished by the course of years: its simplicity kept it going, in the rhythm of time.

In a cupboard in my home I have a pocket watch that belonged to my grandfather and then my father. Somehow, it has never crossed my mind to use it to tell the time.

Gvendur dúllari

Calm?

PAST: A strong breeze from the east initially, then it gradually died down as the day passed, always thin air, strong northwesterly gusts in the light mist, no frost, with drizzle now and then, initially. Now after sunset late this evening it turned to a low easterly with overcast sky, and a light rain hung in the air so that only the moon's face was visible, and mist settled on the slopes as during a sea breeze in summer, and the spray trailed down to the sea.

PRESENT: Rather light northwesterly or changeable winds, patchy cloud.
Occasional light mist in the southeast and in coastal areas of the northeast. Showers likely in the afternoon in the southwest.

PAST: Gvendur *dúllari*.
PRESENT: Sigurður Magnússon.

Paradise Lost

Sigurður Sveinbjörnsson always wrestled with himself and the meaning of life; yes, his focus can be compared to the fate of deserted areas where all roads lead to nowhere – a shadow that stands out from the autumn mask. There is some cold nakedness that surrounds his existence.

On Vacation

First we campaigned fiercely for the Working Hours Act – the right to sleep six hours of twenty-four aboard a side-trawler. Most people were happy with that. Then they introduced vacation that everyone had to take.

Now I'm on vacation.

Afterword

November 24, 2000

My dears

Now, when your grandfather has passed on, much has changed in our life. Words and pictures have held our existence together; the storehouse of ideas and memories has suddenly acquired a new meaning. Your great-grandfather Helgi Magnússon, a blacksmith and merchant in Reykjavík, understood such manifestations well. For instance, he collected pictures of odd people, which are published here in this book. He was constantly leafing through his collection, and never apparently grew tired of speculating about what had happened to the people in the photos. By assembling his collection, he had placed those people in a framework which enabled him to consider their life stories in a nutshell.

Your grandfather Magnús, who was, as you have heard, managing director for many years of the *Harpa* paint company in Reykjavík, received the collection after his father's death, but the pictures had little significance for him. His attitude and feelings towards them were concerned almost entirely with the fact that his father had collected them; and he respected their significance in his father's life.

Two decades ago your grandfather gave me the picture collection. For years I would look at the pictures without understanding their importance for my grandfather and father, or myself. But then there was a damascene moment in my life. Artist Birgir Andrésson, who shared your great-grandfather's interest in vagabonds, held an exhibition at the Reykjavík Academy.

One morning this spring a lot of big portraits of odd people lay against the walls of the long, curving corridor on the fourth floor of the JL House, that houses the Reykjavík Academy. I strode down the 78-metre-long corridor, absorbed in my thoughts. I was observing the pictures in silent astonishment when I saw ahead of me a man knocking a nail into a wall. I realized at once that it was no other than Nobel-prizewinning author Halldór Kiljan Laxness; and I found that I had strayed into a genre that belonged to the local tale tradition, known as *Stories of Odd People*. I approached more closely and greeted Birgir Andrésson, who stepped out of one of the pictures just as I opened my office door and vanished into your great-grandfather's photo album of unusual people.

The exhibition was taken down after your grandfather died last autumn, but the picture album still lies open on my desk. Since then, nothing has been heard of me. And what is more, I doubt whether I shall ever return. You see, my soft spots are manifested best in photography, which has space for the narrow sphere of my thinking. If I were to undertake another long journey, I would have to step out of the frame of the photograph, and who knows what would become of me then? Words and pictures in my life have, in other words, gained new focusses. Today you can look me up in this book and wonder what happened to the people to be found there – just as your great-grandfather once did.

Oh, if your grandfather Magnús only knew....!

May good fortune be with you always. With sincere affection,

SGM

Sources

Parts of the text of this book owe a debt to other writings. I have seen, for instance, a report by the regional physician of Dalir in the archives of the Directorate of Heath (Love-Brandur); in his *Kraftbirtingarhljómur Guðdómsins* (The Sound of Divine Revelation) Magnús Hj. Magnússon expresses his admiration for Símon *Dalaskáld* (poet and friend); the same is true of the speech of the Representative of the People, derived by Halldór Kiljan Laxness partly from the diaries of Magnús Hj. Magnússon, and memorably reworked in *Heimsljós* (World Light) (question and answer session with a representative of the people); Halldór Jónsson of Miðdalsgröf in Strandir was one of those who contemplated the infinity of space, and a text on such thoughts is found in *Bræður af Ströndum* (Brothers from Strandir) (Thought), as is another passage about his material status (List of assets); Tómas Guðmundsson wrote about Ingimundur *fiddle* in *Íslenska örlagaþættir* (Icelandic Tales of Fate) (Poet Tómas Guðmundsson describes a man); in *Harmsaga ævi minnar* (The Tragedy of My Life) Jóhannes Birkiland recounts the tragedy of his life, which includes thoughts on parenting (Health); the culture of emotions is to be found in a letter from a woman to her brother, in the manuscript collection of the National Library of Iceland; in it she compares her temperament to tales about her grandmother, and by her putting down the story in writing it passes from person to person (Thirst for life); accounts of weather conditions are often beautifully worded in old diaries, as discussed in the book *Brothers from Strandir,* while in our time weather reports are found in newspapers (Calm?); Elka Björnsdóttir, a woman laborer in Reykjavík, was surprised when she first saw an airplane flying, and she wrote about it in her diary, which is in the manuscript collection of the National Library (Aviation). Finally, I have had access to accounts by my father and grandfather which have proved useful – not to mention the innumerable works I have had around me all my life.

In the end, life is one big intertextual conglomeration, an unfettered source which will never run dry. For as long as humans look into each other's eyes, associations will arise that are expressed in text and become grist to the mill of further ideas.

Words are so much more than an assemblage of letters making up a whole. They are a construct of life – of the Universe itself.

4   Potential History

The Environment of Egodocuments

A photograph is a memory, a moment frozen in time. Nearly forty years ago I posed for a young woman as she formed in her mind an image of a man, and then sought to portray it in her mind and on paper in the form of lithography. For many years the picture hung on the wall of our home, and later it was put away in my parents' home when I lived abroad. Now it has been brought out once more: it could be part of my autobiography, a fragment of a bigger picture.

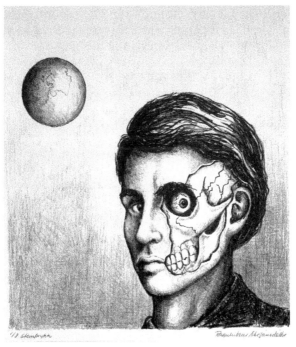

DOI: 10.4324/9781003177661-4

Bonds with people and things are formed and broken, and new bonds are established and broken again. This recurrence is based on the human being's constant attempts to keep hold of their own self. Memories are part of a steady production on which the self is based: memory creation – and memory is the tool we use in our attempts to be what we choose to be.[1]

In 2007, I published a book in Icelandic, *Sögustríð* (History War). The man in the picture on the cover is me! Or, more precisely, I *was* that man. It is, admittedly, rather unusual to place one's own picture on the cover of an academic book, in such a pose. The book is an academic work, but it is also my subjective experience of my field of scholarship, its history and its protocols (liturgy): in a way, a scholarly autobiography. I wanted to underline that aspect of the book by publishing an image of a work which evokes innumerable memories in my mind: part of my past – my self-image. The book is both a critical and a confrontational account of the historiographical development of the discipline of history in Iceland and abroad. At the same time, writing the book gave me the opportunity to evaluate my own academic status in the time I had devoted to history.[2] The general ideas advanced in my previous writing attracted powerful responses from two American historians, Peter N. Stearns and Harvey J. Graff, in the volume, *Sögustríð*. I invited them to write a 'Foreword' (Stearns) and 'Afterword' (Graff) in the book, where they would discuss some of my ideas with the order: 'show no mercy'. And that they did![3]

Shortly after the 40-year-old drawing described above was made, I started to give systematic thought to history. A series of coincidences led to my starting to pursue research based on people's personal testimony – beginning in the 1980s, with interviews with individuals, relating to a work later published in book form by the University of Iceland Institute of History as *Lifshættir í Reykjavík 1930–1940* (Modes of Living in Reykjavík 1930–1940).[4] I then continued, making use of the evidence of authors of autobiographies in the early 1990s when working on my doctoral dissertation in the USA; and finally I used a range of egodocuments of different kinds, such as diaries, letters, handwritten peasant newspapers and scholarly questionnaires, at the end of that decade and to the present. By that time I had started to apply the microhistorical paradigm to my work – a methodology which was highly effective in working with such sources. I may be said to have gradually built up an ideology which was likely to guide me, and possibly others, in academic research. The research problem here partly presented is in a sense the fruit of those 35 years of work and thought.

Icelandic life writing, or the whole genre of egodocuments, can be conveniently broken down into a few broad and overlapping groups: *autobiographies*, where the author is also the main character; *semi-autobiographies*, sometimes referred to as *memoirs*, written by someone other than the main character, based on memories related to the author by the main character; and *conversational books*, where there is a co-operative relationship between author and main character, marked in the text by questions and answers. A database which was compiled a few years ago in connection with my research project on egodocuments identified 1,089 titles published in Iceland between the second half of the 19th century and 2004 that can be categorized as life-writing or egodocuments. Of these, about 85% were written by men.[5] To this material can be added a huge body of other kinds of first-hand sources (diaries, collection of letters, etc.) that, in some cases, have constituted part of Icelandic popular culture over many centuries, such as the 'Local tale tradition.' Considering the whole *genre*, the gender ratio is more consistent with the overall population of the country at the time, than when one only looks at the autobiographical material. All these sources are of diverse kinds, and it is difficult to categorize them into the above-mentioned groups. Within each group we find assorted texts that express all kinds of emotions and events that greatly affect the outcome.

For example, one of the most renowned Icelandic autobiographies is perhaps that of Jóhannes Birkiland (b. 1886), *Harmsaga ævi minnar.*

Hvers vegna varð ég auðnuleysingi (The Tragedy of my Life. Why I Became a Failure).[6] Jóhannes apparently conceals nothing in his account, which must be deemed one of the most interesting autobiographies of that time.[7] He roamed from person to person, place to place, and between continents, never feeling at ease. In a sense the work is an individual's dramatic settling of scores with his own time – the words of a man who had mental issues, yet succeeded in writing a coherent account of his life. For many years, no Icelandic historian felt able to use this autobiography in research, faced by the perceived requirement of veracity. In other words, how would we generally categorize this specific work?

Still, the main character of egodocuments is essentially the same all over the world.[8] But special conditions prevailing in Iceland mean that egodocuments such as autobiographies are quite unusual resources. There is good reason to believe that the tradition of egodocuments is stronger in Iceland than in most other parts of the world.[9] That may be attributable to the strong cultural position of most of the Icelandic population in the 19th century – as literacy rates were exceptionally high – as well as the perennial popularity of saga literature, which continues today.[10] The sagas are, directly and indirectly, an intrinsic part of Icelandic popular culture.

The strong narrative tradition has been widely manifested in Icelandic national life in recent centuries. The art of telling a story, or giving shape to a readable text, has played a major role in Icelandic culture from early times, and the evolution of the tradition is informed by saga literature.[11] The ability to tell a story well was valued: a wanderer who had this skill would generally be welcomed into any home – even if they tended to meet with the disapproval of the authorities. Many autobiographies recount regular visits by vagabonds; and while some may have found such drifters eccentric, and perhaps even disconcerting, they certainly added color to the routine of country life.[12] This was the society that my grandfather grew up in and knew like the back of his hand.

The *kvöldvaka* or winter-eve gathering was a regular element of Icelandic home life until the 20th century. In the dark winter evenings, after all outdoor tasks had been completed, the household would gather in the *baðstofa* (communal living/sleeping loft) to continue their work, mostly woolworking such as spinning and knitting.[13] As they sat at their work, a member of the household would read aloud from some saga, or *rímur* might be chanted. All this was a powerful stimulus to the imagination, as well as enhancing productivity. The evening gathering generally concluded with a reading from a religious text, and singing of hymns. The winter-eve gatherings were influential in many ways, and it was in this setting that children started their education.[14] Here they learned to read and write, as before schools existed in Iceland, parents were responsible for teaching these skills. And they learned to appreciate the value of a good story, and the skill of reading aloud.[15] It is arguable that these factors led to people of all classes feeling the need to sit down and write their own stories.[16] And that became a practical option in the latter half of the 19th century, when writing materials were available quite cheaply, and the publishing sector was expanding fast.[17]

This background to Icelandic egodocuments means that latter-day readers have an unusually good opportunity to address the history of the Icelandic peasantry on their own terms. All over the world, social historians faced the problem that their searches for working-class people's direct testimony about their own lives yield such meager results.[18] Hence the majority of historians resorted to focusing on the institutions that marked out the framework of the daily lives of the peasantry – or the formal structure of society. But there have been departures from that research mode, in very interesting scholarly experiments around the world, known as the *Cultural Turn*. The objective of these is similar to that of research that makes use of egodocuments, i.e. they focus on the *agency*, offering an individual in the past the opportunity to contribute to the study. As I shall discuss below, I have taken a slightly different path to the same goal, mainly by applying the methods of microhistory in historical research.[19] But these have much in common with the *Cultural Turn* in history.

Egodocuments certainly offer the opportunity to gain insight into the world of other people who belong to different social and economic groups and challenge the institutional bias that has characterized social history for many years.[20] Such resources will come into their own when scholars start to analyze them on their own terms, disregarding the requirement of scientific methodology. That is where the methodological opportunities lie.

The historical value of egodocuments have in fact two different dimensions: one is, their idiosyncrasy, uniqueness, almost anomalous nature – which connects well with Ginzburg's sense of microhistory and others at the forefront of that methodology. The other is the 'voice' they give to the normally 'voiceless,' this issue of agency and the subaltern. The connection between these two elements are important in the context of this book, because in another milieu, we might run the risk of divergent aims and goals of both perspectives.

Above I have given an account of the context of autobiographical evolution in my academic environment, and perhaps that may explain the emphases to be found in this volume. I apply my experience in the humanities over the past 25 years in order to shed light on that evolution, just as many historians have done internationally in recent years when historiographical matters are weighed and measured.[21] Of precisely this approach, Spanish historian, Jaume Aurell, remarks in the periodical *History and Theory*: 'I propose to classify these auto-biographies as *interventional* in the sense that these historians use their autobiographies, with a more or less deliberate authorial inten-tion, to participate in, mediate, and intervene in theoretical debates by using the story of their own intellectual and academic itineraries as the source of historiography.'[22] His meaning is that this personal approach opens new paths to the subject, and offers a better oppor-tunity than other approaches for explaining the development of ideas and concepts. Historians who have written their autobiographies 'use autobiographical narratives to contextualize, examine, and define not only their area of specialization but also the very process of writing history.'[23] Aurell points out that this method has been called 'personal scholarship,' 'self-inclusive scholarship,' or 'cross-genre writing.'

As mentioned above, for the past 25 years I have regularly kept a diary, much of which consists of my ideas about history, the past and my wrestling with both in the context of my daily tasks. Not only has the diary itself – these 71 volumes and about 20,000 pages – been my space for all sorts of ideas about history, it has also become a 'thing' that I have treasured like gold. I have kept company with the materi-ality of this particular personal, but at the same time historical, docu-ment, paying attention to the meaning of it as an object – the material nature of the diary. It takes on a scrupulous form of 'thingness' that is loaded with actual power. What is interesting in this context is that I have gained an understanding of the power that resides in the per-sonality governing the writing, the thinking which has found its way onto the page, and the combination of me and my environment which has given rise to the text. It constitutes a distinctive form and textual incarnation where I discuss my diary writing and the meaning of the thoughts that are written down. This emerged with great clarity when I was courting my wife, and at the same time preparing a book about our love, as I recounted above; there I succeeded in putting forward diverse fragments of text, juxtaposed with my own experiences, thus creating a text that stood for a certain rare entity. That may have been because I place the thoughts which are found on the diary pages into a specific textual space; where I write, and how I feel when processing my materials, is part of my narrative. My handwriting varies noticeably from one time to another, which leads me to contemplate how I was feeling, and what my circumstances were, when each entry was written.

I consider how I preserve the diaries from day to day, what will happen to them after my time – and people who feature in the diaries have even expressed views on what should happen to them. I found, for instance, that I had to reassure my wife by means of a formal document stating what would happen to my diaries after my time. They will be entrusted to the Manuscript Department of the National Library after my death, and I have placed them under her authority for her lifetime (so that she may decide whether anybody is granted access to them). I am sure that family members and friends have had concerns about what may have found its way into the diary, although no one has mentioned the matter to me directly. Everyone who knows me is aware that I keep a diary, and I have not sought to conceal the work that has gone into it – as witness an article on the back page of Iceland's largest newspaper in 2019. Thus this archive has been a living element of my life and how it has progressed – a part of the formation of my ideas about history and the past, and my own life.

In this volume I have, in the same way, used my experience as a historian in the field for many years to reflect on the importance of approaching one's subject matter with an open mind. That is really what potential history is all about. This approach has nothing to do with the 'what if' brand of history. On the contrary, it is based upon opening new paths to the subjects of the past, which have not been trodden before, as the traditional method of searching for sources has placed limits on such scholarship.

It is fair to say that I have, throughout my career, been striving to shake off these shackles in some sense, and the keeping of my diary, described above, is clear evidence of that. The diary has inspired me with the desire to approach my subjects from some other direction than conventional history has permitted. The microhistorical approach within academia has assuredly also been a path to that destination.

The potentialities for interpretations and studies of uncomfortable subjects are almost inexhaustible, using the autobiographical focus. What is most important, however, is that one can take archives which have been staring at one for decades, and work with them in a new and enlightening manner – at the same time as one's own life becomes an historical source. 'Recent developments in cultural studies,' argues

Morgunbladid

FIMMTUDAGUR 7. MAÍ 128. DAGUR ÁRSINS 2020

Hugsanabók að dagbók

● **Sigurður Gylfi hefur skrifað 20.000 blaðsíður í 70 dagbækur**

Steinþór Guðbjartsson
steinthor@mbl.is

Sigurður Gylfi Magnússon, náms-
brautarformaður í sagnfræði og
prófessor í sagnfræði- og
heimspekideild Háskóla Íslands,
hefur unnið mikið með dagbækur í
rannsóknum sínum og varð sú vinna
til þess að hann fór sjálfur að skrifa
hjá sér helstu viðburði líðandi
stundar 1996. „Síðan þá er ég búinn
að skrifa um 20.000 blaðsíður og er á
70. bókinni," segir hann.

Skömmu eftir að Sigurður Gylfi
kom heim frá námi í Bandaríkjunum
spurði hann nemendur í námskeiði
um persónulegar heimildir, sem
hann kenndi í sagnfræðinni í HÍ,
hverjir hefðu haldið dagbækur í
lengri eða skemmri tíma og honum
til undrunar var það stór hluti. „Ég
hugsaði með mér að ég þyrfti að
prófa þetta sjálfur."

Námskeið um heimildir

Til að byrja með skrifaði Sigurður
Gylfi niður hugmyndir, sem hann
ætlaði að vinna úr í rannsóknum
sínum. „Ég kallaði þetta hugsana-
bók," segir hann. Tveimur árum síð-
ar byrjaði hann að halda reglulega
dagbók. „Ég var frjáls í forminu og
skrifaði þegar mér þótti ástæða til.
Á þessum tíma var ég formaður
Sagnfræðingafélagsins og stjórnar
Reykjavíkurakademíunnar og skrifaði einkum um fundi og hvar ég ætti
að vera hina og þessa stundina.
Hægt og bítandi fór ég að skrifa um
mitt persónulega líf, þó að stofninn
hafi áfram verið unninn út frá rann-
sóknarhugmyndum í sagnfræðinni."

Dagbækur hafa lengi heillað Sig-
urð Gylfa og honum finnst til dæmis
merkilegt að alþýðufræðimaðurinn
Sighvatur Grímsson Borgfirðingur
hafi haldið dagbók í 67 ár, skrifað
15.000 blaðsíður á 19. öld. „Það sér-
staka við mín dagbókarskrif er að ég
lít aldrei til baka, fletti bókunum
ekki til að rifja eitthvað upp nema
brýn þörf sé til þess. Ég les þær
aldrei mér til skemmtunar heldur
eru þær fyrir mig í núinu, þegar ég
skrifa; hugleiðingar um andartakið
sem líður."

Þessa dagana er verið að kynna
grunn- og framhaldsnámið í sagnfræði við HÍ, meðal annars á Youtu-
be, og segist Sigurður Gylfi finna
fyrir miklum áhuga nemenda á per-

Minningar Ljósmyndir hjálpa við að rifja upp liðna tíð. Sigurður Gylfi
Magnússon og Alvía fagna Íslandsmeistaratitlinum í fótbolta í fyrra.

sónulegum heimildum eins og dag-
bókum. „Þær veita ákveðna sýn inn í
fortíðina sem er áhugaverð," segir
hann. Í því sambandi bendir hann á
að í fyrra hafi hann kennt nám-
skeiðið „Er eitthvað á minnið að
treysta?" „Þá velti ég því fyrir mér
hvers virði þessar persónulegu
heimildir eru, getum við treyst
þeim? Ég fékk nemendurna til að
skrifa sjálfsævisögu sína – einhvern
hluta hennar – og þáttur í verkefn-
inu var að skýra út fyrir lesand-
anum hvaða tæki þeir notuðu til að
rifja hluti upp. Þar komu dagbækur
að gagni. Málið er að dagbókin er
orðin virt heimild í rannsóknum sem
lúta að hversdagsupplifunum fólks
og hvernig alþýðan réði ráðum sínum á 18., 19. og 20. öld."

Þegar faðir Sigurður Gylfa and-

aðist árið 2000 aðstoðaði hann móð-
ur sína við að flytja. Þá segist hann
hafa fundið 100 bréfa bunka, sem
hann hafi sent þeim á fyrstu þremur
árunum í Bandaríkjunum. Þetta hafi
í raun verið eins konar dagbókarskrif og þegar hann hafi flett bréf-
unum hafi hann áttað sig á því að
margt var gleymt en rifjaðist upp
við lesturinn. „Minningaskrif, eins
og dagbækur og bréf, eru mikil-
vægar heimildir rétt eins og ljósmyndir eða kvikmyndir, auk þess
sem staðir og lykt geta rifjað upp
minningar," segir Sigurður Gylfi.
„Þetta er það sem við kennum í
sagnfræðinni, að vinna með margs
konar flóknar heimildir til þess meðal annars að vara sig á blekkingum
og falsfréttum sem vaða yfir heim-
inn og hafa lengi gert!"

Jaume Aurell, 'suggest that cultural practices and products – such as history books – are highly performative: they *construct* as they *recount*.'[24] He goes on to point out that historians have turned to autobiography '... simply to say things they feel they cannot say within the framework of academia.'[25] And Jaume Aurell concludes this discussion with the following declaration, which I feel is in accord with my own thinking and ideas as presented in this book:

> More specifically, I argue that interventional autobiography becomes a historiographical laboratory for the historians who practice it: their experiments with history *outside* themselves have drawn them to explore the history *inside* themselves, turning this process from objectivity to subjectivity into an operation of both historical and historiographical (that is, theoretical) writing.[26]

The Archive – Personal Expression

What is an archive? That is, essentially, the question at the heart of the discourse in this book. I have approached the archive as a phenomenon which possesses the quality of being able to tell a story – really, any story. By this I mean that each individual has a different sense of the archive they have in their hands. That is the origin of many ego-documents which were discussed above. Each and every writer has some kind of archive to work from, when they write their stories, their reflections on life and existence.[27]

Antoinette Burton, editor of *Archive Stories,* wrote in her introduction to the book, about collection and storage of sources:

> Of course, archives – that is, traces of the past collected either intentionally or haphazardly as 'evidence' – are by no means limited to official spaces or state repositories. They have been housed in a variety of unofficial sites since time immemorial. From the Rosetta stone to medieval tapestry to Victorian house museums to African body tattoos, scholars have been 'reading' historical evidence off of any number of different archival incarnations for centuries, though the extent to which a still quite positivist contemporary historical profession (both in the West and outside it) recognizes all such traces as legitimate archival sources is a matter of some debate.[28]

My grandfather's photographic archive is indeed an excellent example of the problem stated here by Antoinette Burton: what may be deemed an archive? One of the contributors to the book under Burton's editorship clearly establishes that the meaning of *archive* is variable from one time to another:

> While history can indeed be found in the 'archive,' the place and shape of that history was imagined differently at different times; the institution of the Archives was itself a testament of particular regimes of power and knowledge, each marked by particular commitments to and rhetorics of secrecy of publicity.[29]

Is the assemblage of photographs – the archive – with which I have been working in this book an archive of the kind described by Burton above? We, the representatives of three generations – my grandfather, my father and I – each certainly approached this specific archive differently – each in his own way. The trick is to understand the mirroring that takes place every time the archive is examined and analyzed. The archive is a reflection of some reality, which often has nothing to do with the material of which the archive apparently consists when it is examined *in toto*: the photos are of different provenances; they are taken at specific moments, capturing events which vary in significance for the people depicted. And for the readers of this book, my grandfather's archive acquires an entirely new meaning for each and every person who examines the photographs and considers their significance. The reason is simply that we observe the world through our own eyes, and we each see different things in each snapshot. Each image is, certainly, a world of its own; the details of the images provide material for our thinking and narrative; and as we connect that narrative to other images and their content, a vision of part reality takes form. The pictures that constitute this archive of my grandfather give rise to endless textual cogitation.[30]

I chose to address this specific archive because it had significance for me, and also by chance. Hence I succeeded in evading the purposive power of the formal archive: how they have been compiled, the principles on which items were collected, etc. US historian, Peter Fritzsche, puts this issue well when he points out:

> The archive was not simply constituted as a powerful way to contain the past but developed in relationship to a past that was regarded as fragmented, distant, and otherwise difficult to hold on to. The archive produced certain histories, but, at the same time, certain ways of looking at and believing to have experienced history also produced archives. If most conceptions of the archive

emphasize how the archive has shaped history, I want to examine how history has shaped the archive.[31]

My method is that sometimes I recount only what I think I see, creating a narrative from the picture – a microhistorical narrative – while sometimes I consider what is happening in the photograph, and I may even place it in a historical context. Sometimes the text has little or nothing to do with the photograph, which becomes a kind of backdrop for my own personal thoughts – but often grounded in some small detail in the picture. The outcome is texts which conform with Jane Bennett's ideas, when she asks what 'things' may be concerned with, instead of an analysis of exactly what they are.[32] We may say, in fact, that the text that accompanies the photographs is first and foremost in a dialogue with the poetical or subjective to be found there – and that material is certainly a striking element of each picture, and important source for our inspiration. The dialogue is between the person residing in the heart of the writer (or reader) and the people in the photographs.

It is possible, however, to approach the material in quite a different manner – i.e. to connect with the subject on the basis of the objective reality to be found there and the relationship between objects and people in the pictures.[33] An informal statistical analysis of the archive, for instance, reveals that the photographs show 79 people – of whom nine are clearly identifiable as women – in a leading or supporting role in each picture; in addition at least 54 are wearing some kind of headgear – hats or caps. One woman covers her head with a shawl, and nine men are bare-headed. The photos show at least 12 walking canes, five liquor bottles or kegs, four bicycles, two motor vehicles, four brooches, a wine glass or goblet, a horse and whip, a pile of bits of wood – to which I make reference, along with a rat and a trap – many chairs and a number of tables, a pocket watch, a shield and spear, a broom, several medals, a book, a hairband, musical instruments, a large clock, and various buildings... and in one picture possibly a travelling trunk.

This is, of course, wonderfully rich material for working with the idea of composite characters – characters made up of both human and non-human agents/actants. Obviously, hats were a fashion item, but that is not the whole story. A hat said a lot about the person wearing the hat. Different people wore various kinds of hats and caps. New graduates from the high school wore a specific kind of white cap. The king of Denmark and Iceland, on an official visit, wore a white cap too – but it was not a high-school graduate's cap. By the same token, not all males were lame and infirm in olden times, yet they still carried a walking cane. Motor vehicles are scarcely seen, liquor is omnipresent, and the pictures manifest a specific aspect of Icelandic life: people meeting by chance and chatting. Almost everyone, we may say, wore a hat or cap and walked with a cane. Everything else was individual. But it would often set the tone for the ambiance of each picture.

What is the meaning of this observation? Can the photographs be interpreted however we please – are they in truth a *tabula rasa*, although there are both people and objects in them? What can safely be affirmed is that we see composite beings in every picture – and of course it is the objects, in their stability, which imbue the people in the photographs with certain qualities which are hard to ignore. Nor do I do so, and thus I remain true to the source – the archive – because I take account, after all, of the ontological context entailed by each image. The point is, however, that the ontological context changes with each individual who examines the pictures – they will always add something new to every image. That addition is, however, based in the ontological state entailed by the frozen moment – and in that way the source as a phenomenon, and the archive in its totality, have importance for the historian. I do want to point out that, in a sense though, this subverts the idea of a photograph as a frozen moment, because it foregrounds the image-viewer relation which is dynamic and pregnant with duration.[34]

What would be your approach to these pictures? What composite beings are in these pictures, to your mind? Thus one could ask each and every reader, and each would reach their own independent conclusions. But they are not only composites – they are also fragmented. Most of the images depict just a fragment of these multi-composite people: sometimes only the face, and as a rule with a hat or some other addition, such as a liquor keg. The fact is that photographs are, obviously, so very situational, i.e. they capture and preserve moments which are often swallowed up in the noise that is a by-product of documentation of other kinds: official documents, egodocuments such as diaries – not to mention archaeological data collections or museum collections of all kinds. Profusion is characteristic of such archives, in which the unique feature tends to get lost. A photograph freezes a single moment, which may be carefully planned and posed, or equally well a random event from the whirlwind of time. What is particularly interesting about these moments is that they focus on compositions. The photographs provide us, at least, with the chance to consider more carefully these compositions created by people, things and their surroundings. It is something like those rare moments in music where a kind of perfection exists in one moment, one chord – yet generally vanishes as soon as it has passed. The same may be said of almost every field of human existence: sometimes the world simply attains perfection! One of these moments in time might be called 'Manifestations of Poverty,' and contains a unique archive of photographs taken in 1930–1945 by bank employee, Sigurður Guttormsson, of the Westman Islands. The archive comprises a total of 230 photographs of poor people's homes, taken all over Iceland. The archive, which Sigurður presented to the Confederation of Labour in an effort to spur it to action regarding housing for the poor, now in the National Archives.[35]

Let us return to what I was considering above: what is the significance of all the objects that feature in the photographs, and are necessary and essential participants in the objective-human compositions presented in the pictures? They are canes, hats, chairs, clothing, brooches, tables, a clock and so on. Museums are crammed with such objects, but there the objects lack the context offered by the compositions in the photographs. A cane in a glass cabinet in a museum may assuredly be a fine piece of craftsmanship, it may have historical significance (Churchill's cane, for instance), while a photograph in which a cane participates – not to mention many photographs with canes, as in this book (a total of 12) – is a situational composition which brings history to life – we may perhaps call them a subject for microhistory – *par excellence!*[36] And going back to John Tagg's work, sited earlier, on photography and the extent to which such objects might – *sometimes* – be seen as staging props, helping the viewer to 'read' the photograph in a particular way, one is convinced of its importance.

Finally, it should be stated that historians tend to have reservations about photographs. In his interesting book, *Eyewitnessing*, British historian, Peter Burke, says:

Needless to say, the use of the testimony of images raises many awkward problems. Images are mute witnesses and it is difficult to translate their testimony into words. They may have been intended to communicate a message of their own, but historians not infrequently ignore it in order to read pictures "between the lines, "and learn something that the artists did not know they were teaching. There are obvious dangers in this procedure. To use the evidence of images safely, let alone effectively, it is necessary – as in the case of other kinds of source – to be aware of its weaknesses.[37]

The Archive – Definition!

In the book *The Archive Project*, the authors commence their introductory chapter with the following definition: 'Broadly, archival research is concerned with a collection of documents – texts of different kinds, including but not confined to words on paper, visual materials or physical objects; and it involves analysing and interpreting these so as to explore a particular topic or question or concern.'[38] They go on to demonstrate that often certain parts of a specific archive are especially scrutinized, or that a broader approach becomes the historian's subject. They point out that the path to the archive can be complicated, and that its content is not necessarily some kind of embodiment of the past, as much that relates to the archive happens in the present. The archive is reshuffled by the keepers of the material, and made accessible in accord with the needs of the present day. Other material is packed up and put away for decades, without ever being seen by the public. And it is true to say that the content of the archive always reflects the present, although long-ago events are being addressed in scholars' research. We must not forget that items from the original archive have been discarded, and it will have been thinned out for various reasons – that is simply one aspect of the process of conservation. And it cannot be ignored that many archives are subject to strict requirements – rules and standards formulated long ago, which have a formative impact on the possibilities for using them.

The authors go on to say that opinions differ on why archival research is important, mentioning two main views:

> One, the most simple but with profound implications, is that 'the past' is a shorthand for everything that has come before and made us, our lives and the societies we live in, what they are. So understanding even small parts of the past can give us a handle on things in the present and possibly aspects of the future, too. Another, and related, response is that the present and the future are uncontrollable, while the remaining traces of the past, including the near-past that contemporary archiving is concerned with, are finite and can be made at least provisionally known, albeit with many ifs and buts.[39]

In other words, archives are storage places of knowledge and culture, if we take the argument of the authors of *The Archive Project* seriously, which scholars strive to approach using their academic tools, in order to acquire an opportunity to gain access to the past. The question is simply this: what past is it that is brought out by today's scholars? The archive as an historical phenomenon is primarily a storage place for knowledge about the formal and regulated: as a rule, archives record the development of the nation state and the dominant powers in society. The status of the archive becomes, however, outrageous and descends into chaos when a scholar sets to work, for instance, in former colonial territories, and turns their attention to the powerless, in whatever form.[40] In such cases, new means of studying the past and existing sources must often be sought; means which have not always met with the approval of conventional history. The argument of the authors of *The Archive Project* ignores the fact that archives – although about preserving the past – are really about carrying that past over into an indefinite future. Archives are as future-oriented as they are past-oriented. Which means, in a sense, they are less about controlling the past as controlling the present and future through their preservationist practices.

The authors of *The Archive Project* point out that the archive has a remarkable place in society, due to the fact that it becomes a storage place for the idea of the death of all those who lived through the archive! The phenomenon thus serves to remind us of the transience of life; in other words, it confirms one thing for sure: that we will all die. Yet, despite this philosophical significance of the archive, it functions first and foremost as a storage place for memories, material left behind by living people or phenomena of the past. That fact is by no means simple: on the contrary it gives rise to innumerable difficulties in handling the archive. The authors of the book maintain that people of the present time seek both to catalogue the archive and to organize it, just like their own lives; and hence the archive becomes a mechanism for understanding existence.

Many historians approach the phenomenon *archive* as a gateway to the past; within is to be found 'material' that has not been lost. The authors discuss *inter alia* British historian, Carolyn Steedman, and her interpretation of the archive. 'Her take on this is that it is precisely its absence that feeds imagination and analysis, that scholarly activity of filling the gaps between the traces that remain. It is the very incompleteness that moves understanding forward ...'[41] That fact – that 'obviously deconstructionist vein' – makes the archive an unusually alluring subject, which demands a hugely extensive approach to the phenomenon *per se*. It is probably fair to say that this fact is precisely a feature of the ideas of many microhistorians about the work of the historian: to recognize that the sources have little to tell us about that past, and that it is important to identify the gaps in our knowledge

– that it is just as important to identify the lacunae in our knowledge as to address the fragments of knowledge themselves.[42]

I can assuredly agree once more with what Antoinette Burton says when she describes her work as '... motivated, in other words, by our conviction that history is not merely a project of fact-retrieval ... but also a set of complex processes of selection, interpretation, and even creative invention – processes set in motion by, among other things, one's personal encounter with the archive, the history of the archive itself, and the pressure of the contemporary moment on one's reading of what is to be found there.'[43] This is certainly an important declaration, which undermines historians' conventional approach to their subjects. Some acknowledge this, while others carry on regardless, continuing to approach the archive as a reliable way to the secrets of the past.

Niamh Moore, Andrea Salter, Liz Stanley and Maria Tamboukou, the authors of *The Archive Project* as stated above, provide detailed explanations of diverse views relating to collecting, the organization of collections, analysis of the material they contain and other uses of the archive. We may say, though with some simplification, that all this discourse is grounded in two arguments, or rather two approaches to the phenomenon *archive.*

In the first place, scholars maintain that archives '... are incomplete as well as partial; they hold fragments of traces, representations of representations, and as Steedman (2001: 45) has put it, "You find nothing in the archive but stories caught half way through." What then can be known and how? Can knowledge reside in, be derived from, the fragmentary and partial?'[44] The authors are not prepared to accept this interpretation of the place of the archive, and they reject it entirely, unlike Steedman and Burton.

In the second place – and now we come to the above-mentioned authors' understanding of the archive – is the idea that the archive does in fact have an important role to play in guiding our knowledge toward the objective of illuminating the past, applying the tools of academic knowledge:

> Ethically and intellectually, we conclude with some firmness that what matters are the lives and events of people of the past (and the present) and making some kind of sense of these. Relatedly, we see the feelings and experiences of researchers as largely irrelevant except in relation to how understanding and knowledge are produced, and here we think the analytical and interpretive processes involved are certainly important and to be taken critically appreciative note of.[45]

Here they refer to the situation that, due to the prior arguments that archives are simply an assemblage of fragments which are hard to understand and piece together, scholarship has increasingly turned to what may be termed 'archival stories.' These are based upon the researcher's experience of the material – an anthropological study of a kind, where the scholar recounts their experience and feeling for the sources.[46] This may be said, in a sense, to be the approach I apply in this book (in some form), which was addressed in *Archive Stories*, cited above.[47] The approach is based upon the assumption that the archive is so fragmentary and limited that the researcher must put him/herself in the position of both exploring what comes into his/her hands, and at the same time working with the gaps in knowledge. The gaps are, in other words, no less important than what is known. The authors of *The Archive Project*, on the other hand, reach a different conclusion: 'As this indicates, we are certainly not against either ethnography or reflexivity as such, but find the valorisation of feeling and a heroic version of the researcher's subjectivity unhelpful.'[48]

The authors take the view that it is one thing to address the limitations of the archive, in whatever form, and another 'to remain immersed in self.' Their idea is that it is important never to take one's eye off the people and events the researcher intends to study; that the scholar's objective must surely always be to strive to understand what people's lives were like in the past. Hence Niamh Moore, Andrea Salter, Liz Stanley and Maria Tamboukou may perhaps be classified as 'documentarists,' i.e. scholars who take the view that the past is past and cannot be recreated, while knowledge of it may be structured and approached by the study of documents – traces of diverse kinds.[49] The question that remains unanswered is how such study is best pursued.

Heterotopia (Space) – Spaces of Otherness (No-Place)

So what is this study about, that is based upon the archive that is my grandfather's collection of photographs? How can we define it, and the approach on which it is based? The non-autobiography is largely free of the conventional endeavors of the historian, who would leave no stone unturned in the effort to dig up all possible information about each photograph, the people portrayed, and the photographers. In that case, of course, the principle would be to analyze time and place, working on the basis of known factors derived from a range of sources, and contextualize appropriately. Instead of following that conventional path, the material is here discussed in a highly enigmatic manner – really, as if the photograph and its content might have nothing to do with me. My focus is still more on the collective impact of the archive on my grand-father, my father and myself. The way to the archive and the people in the photographs is thus through the enigmatic – a 'reality' that doesn't exist! The 'biography' of the object, the archive as an object, is the approach on which I focus, while also promoting the random elements of the archive by telling the story relating to each picture, reflecting my impressions of the photograph at the time.[50]

Foucault's concept of *hétérotopie*, 'a place of difference/otherness' – a space which participants find almost disturbing, and incompatible with the societal and ideological paths of experience, may perhaps serve best to place this work among the academic flora.[51] Historian Nile Green of UCLA in the USA makes the following points in a paper in *American Historical Review* 2018: 'A heterotopia, then, contradicts, challenges, and potentially overturns the familiar assumptions of those who enter it.'[52] Green maintains that the value of the heterotopia consists primarily in the researcher feeling that they are discovering something new, the process of equivocal experience 'as distinct from ideological uniformity,' as he puts it. Heterotopia leads to a certain disruption of conventional approaches, and may be described as a 'state of multiple possibilities rather than predetermined outcomes.'[53] Heterotopia is a space which is part of 'the other' which is far removed from the idea behind consensus; it is rather part of the contradictions we find in everyday life, the intense relationship between two or more parties, and can even be disturbing when someone faces its conse-quences. It is a space with many different layers of meanings.

My grandfather withdrew from his conventional daily space, and disappeared into the world of the photographs – a different space – which provided him with the opportunity to examine them in quite a different light than would otherwise have been possible. He lived in a large house in the center of Reykjavík from 1902 until his death in the 1950s. He was in the habit of waking up very early and going down to the basement to start the boiler that would heat the entire house. Off the boiler-room he had a room of his own, where no one was permitted to enter uninvited. On a table there was the photograph album, which he never seemed to tire of leafing through. He almost seem to have found there a *space of otherness (no-place)*.

To my father and me, it was simply an assemblage of photographs that had no particular significance, except perhaps a sentimental one. It was not until later that the character of the photographs became quite different from what I had experienced before – when I succeeded in connecting them with each other, and at the same time disconnect-ing them from the reality which had informed my thinking.

At that point this archive became a heterotopia – in a sense a contradiction to all I knew – material torn from the context of rules and law. I define heterotopias as different places which provide either an unsettling or an alternative representation of spatial and social relations. I see heterotopias as laboratories for experimenting with new ways of ordering the archive. And that is precisely how I approach this archive of photographs collected by my grandfather. It thus becomes a path into a field previously unknown to me, which may be defined as a heterotopia. I realize that this argument might raise the paradox that in ordering the archive, you might be seen taming or domesticating this heterotopia – negating its very being, but that is not my intension.

How could it be otherwise, on closer scrutiny? This archive came into existence in much the same way as almost all other archives we know. Individual objects are accumulated almost at random over a long period. Each item in the archive – each photograph – originated even more randomly, when someone got the idea of taking photographs of these unfortunates, often living on the margins of society. My grandfather is said to have acquired the photographs in various ways: he did not take the pictures. The randomness of the origin of the photographs, and the absence of connection between each photograph and my grandfather's 'archive' is almost absolute. That is not changed by the fact that certain aspects of the material are constant: the archive consists solely of photographs, all of which are black-and-white, all from a certain period, and depicting similar characters – marginalized people. These factors make the assemblage into an archive. In these circumstances, the question inevitably arises: what kind of archive is this, and what can be done with it? One thing is for sure: it is located in a situation that may be termed a heterotopia: enigmatic, full of paradoxes, leading to a disruption of prior values.

Affirmative Humanities

Polish historian, Ewa Domańska, wrote a paper a few years ago in which she dealt with the concept of 'affirmative humanities,' as mentioned above. The paper is based on ideas about the future of the humanities, which must counterbalance the Doomsday prognostications of postmodernism. She wanted to make an attempt to escape the negative discourse about the world which is widely felt to be a consequence of postmodern turmoil, and perhaps to approach her subjects in a new way, and by other means than those applied by scholars hitherto. Her paper had striking relevance to the experiment pursued in this book, in a 'non-autobiography' – Soft Spots. When she refers to postmodernism, she is also alluding to related concepts such as post-structuralism, deconstruction, textualism, narrativism, culturalism and psychoanalysis – all concepts that had an impact on how research and analysis was carried out 'and the theoretical frameworks that set out the themes and approaches explored in humanities research.'[54] And she also considers what has changed in the past ten years: what fundamental changes have taken place that have influenced humanity over the past ten years or so, such as

> ... the formation of a new paradigm that is variously described as bio-, ego- and/or posthumanities or non-anthropocentric and post-European (or non-Western) humanities, while making this question relevant to the issues affecting the contemporary world that are now not only of a global but also planetary nature (genocide, terrorism, migration, global capitalism, crisis of democracy, biopolitics, poverty, genetic engineering, environmental pollution, climate change and natural disasters).[55]

Ewa Domańska argues that all these turns came up with ideas about how the future can react to all the problems facing the world. *Potential history* is something she, and philosopher, Rosi Braidotti, argue for in their writing.[56] Domańska calls it *affirmative humanities*. But what is that? Domańska replies by pointing out that her understanding of the phenomenon is as follows:

> An affirmative humanities is not about affirming and protecting a traditional concept of life. Instead, it is about support, empowerment, stimulating development, and constructing space for creating individual and collective identity/subjectivity; about creating potentiality (*potentia*) for actions contributing to designing futures within a framework of 'sustainable development'.[57]

Affirmative humanities is thus a forward-looking ideology which rejects the negative and focuses on the positive in the future by abolishing old variables which we tend to use for comparison. The identifying features of affirmative humanities are thus a range of factors with which we are familiar from scholarship and science, such as to reject the egocentric human individual, that we often define as an assemblage of human and non-human persons. In other words, Domańska takes the concept to mean 'knowledge of co-existence in conflict ... that is future-oriented and works to neutralise both anthropocentrism as well as eurocentrism, which, until now, have been the dominant modes of constructing knowledge about the world and humanity.'[58]

The method Domańska seeks to apply is grounded in 'positive' reading of historical sources, and an attempt to avoid 'various forms of insufficiency, such as incoherence, contradiction, logical errors and weakness of argumentation.' According to Domańska, philosopher, Elizabeth Grosz, maintained that this was very much in tune with a male way of reading historical sources. By pursuing research in this manner, she says, it would probably be possible to bring out the potential of any historical situation that has previously been overlooked. Grosz, however, advocates abandoning a critical approach, and she is more an advocate of 'an uncritical affirmative reading,' with which Domańska does not agree. She wishes, on the contrary, to uphold all the strict standards of source criticism or information evaluation, while pursuing such studies by a positive affirmative method.

These ideas give rise to what may be termed 'potential history,' which I have indeed used as the title of this section. Its aim is reconciliatory, as Domańska points out; it prizes out of the past 'unrealised potentials, with this being a condition for creating a different future.'[59] The key, to Domańska, is the creation of archives made up of material that is conducive to a new approach on the principles of affirmative humanities. I would maintain, on the other hand, that it is possible to take 'old' archives, like the one assembled by my grandfather, and re-read them, applying the method offered by potential history – free of the requirement to seek out something specific in the photographs (as traditional history generally requires of its followers), instead approaching the entire archive as an entity which can point us toward a 'positive' image of the future. As Domańska puts it, the imagination is a certain basis for potential history, 'as it draws attention to the role of the imagination in knowledge-making and the legitimacy of shaping the imagination of young practitioners of historical knowledge.'[60]

I should not say that I want to 're-read' my grandfather's archive, since what is interesting about it is that it is somewhat heterotopic, that it defies the norms of traditional archives and in that sense, the potential history it offers is built-in. The link between the archive as I understand it and potential history is obvious; seeing archives as ways of shaping the future, not simply preserving the past, since they are ultimately about the kind of pasts I want to project into the future.

My path in this book, toward the text that belonged to my grandfather's archive, is by no means as ambitious as the one taken by Ewa

Domańska. She set out to apply the idea of affirmative humanities as a means of resolving conflicts between warring factions: instead of focusing on differences, it would be possible to approach the subject on the basis of the common values of the conflicting parties. I, on the other hand, seek only to try to bring out what the personal viewpoint offers: a far more detailed view of the world than has hitherto been deemed possible by the scholarly world. Here it is essential to give the personal experience free rein, to bring out from the depths of consciousness an ambiance that would otherwise be sidelined. The autobiographical approach manifested in this book is something that historians have increasingly resorted to, seeking to understand difficult subjects from the past on the basis of their own experiences. Here we find what may be termed potential history, a new path into the past which scholars have been wary of pursuing.[61]

It is of great value to give free rein to the view that material may be approached using new methods which have not featured hitherto in the scholarly environment. The idea behind this act has been to explore how an archive like the one created by my grandfather can open up a view into the past through what we may call *potential history*. In that way we can embark on a dialogue with both past and future, based on the values and knowledge at our disposal – in a space which may be called a *heterotopia (space) – space of otherness (no-place)*. Thus potential history becomes a scholarly approach which may make a difference.

Notes

1 On memory, see for example the following: Maurice Halbwachs, *On Collective Memory* (Chicago: University of Chicago Press, 1992 [1914]); Pierre Nora, 'Between Memory and History: *Les Lieux de Mémoire*.' *Representations* 26 (Spring 1989), 7–25; *Memory and History in the Twentieth-Century Australia*. Kate Darian-Smith and Paula Hamilton, eds. (Melbourne: Oxford University Press, 1994); Michael S. Roth, *The Ironist's Cage: Memory, Trauma and the Construction of History* (New York: Columbia University Press, 1995); Nancy Wood, *Vectors of Memory. Legacies of Trauma in Postwar Europe* (Oxford: Berg Publishers, 1999); Susan A. Crane, "*AHR Forum*: Writing the Individual Back into Collective Memory," *American Historical Review* 102 (December 1997), 1372–1385.
2 Sigurður Gylfi Magnússon, *Sögustríð. Greinar og frásagnir um hugmyndafræði* (Reykjavík: Miðstöð einsögurannsókna and ReykjavíkurAkademían, 2007).
3 Harvey J. Graff, 'History's War of the Wor(l)ds,' *Sögustríð. Greinar og frásagnir um hugmyndafræði* (Reykjavík: Miðstöð einsögurannsókna and ReykjavíkurAkademían, Reykjavík, 2007), 475–481; Peter N. Stearns,

'Debates About Social History and its Scope,' *Sögustríð. Greinar og frásagnir um hugmyndafræði* (Reykjavík: Miðstöð einsögurannsókna and ReykjavíkurAkademían, 2007), 17–21.

4 Sigurður Gylfi Magnússon, *Lífshættir í Reykjavík, 1930–1940.* Sagnfræðirannsóknir 7 (Reykjavík: Bókaútgáfa Menningarsjóðs, 1985).

5 For the various genres of life writing and egodocuments in Iceland, see Sigurður Gylfi Magnússon, *Fortíðardraumar*; and also Sigurður Gylfi Magnússon, *Sjálfssögur.*

6 Jóhannes Birkiland, *Harmsaga ævi minnar. Hvers vegna ég varð auðnuleysingi* (Reykjavík: Höfundur, 1945).

7 I used part of his text in a chapter on the non-autobiography called 'Health' earlier in this book.

8 A large number of works may be cited which bear witness to the prolific discourse on autobiographies. See, e.g. James S. Amelang, 'Vox Populi: Popular Autobiographies as Sources for Early Modern Urban History,' *Urban History* 20 (1993), 30–42; Arianne Baggerman, 'Autobiography and Family Memory in the Nineteenth Century,' *Egodocuments and History. Autobiographical Writing in its Social Context since the Middle Ages.* Rudolf M. Dekker, ed. (Hilversum: Verloren, 2002), 161–175; *Alternative Identities. The Self in Literature, History, Theory.* Linda Marie Brooks, ed. (New York: Routledge, 1995); Jill Ker Conway, *When Memory Speaks: Reflections on Autobiography* (New York: Alfred A. Knopf, Inc., 1998); Mark A. Conway, *Theoretical Perspectives on Autobiographical Memory* (Dordrecht: Springer, 1992); *True Relations. Essays on Autobiography and the Post-modern.* Thomas C. Couser and Joseph Fichtelberg eds. (Westport, Conn.: Praeger, 1998); *Egodocuments and History. Autobiographical Writing in its Social Context since the Middle Ages.* Rudolf M. Dekker, ed. (Hilversum: Verloren, 2002); Rudolf M. Dekker, *Childhood, Memory and Autobiography in Holland from Golden Age to Romanticism* (London: Palgrave, 1999); *The Culture of Autobiography: Constructions of Self-Representation.* Robert Folkenflik, ed. (Stanford: Stanford University Press, 1993); *Imagined Childhoods. Self and Society in Autobiographical Accounts.* Marianne Gullestad, ed. (Oslo: Scandinavian University Press, 1996); *Encyclopedia of Life Writing. Autobiographical and Biographical Forms* I-II. Margaretta Jolly, ed. (London: Routledge, 2002); Bruce M. Ross, *Remembering the Personal Past. Descriptions of Autobiographical Memory* (New York: Oxford University Press, 1991); David C. Rubin, *Remembering our Past: Studies in Autobiographical Memory* (Cambridge: Cambridge University Press, 1996).

9 See: Davíð Ólafsson, 'Wordmongers: Post-Medieval Scribal Culture and the Case of Sighvatur Grímsson,' PhD. diss., University of St. Andrews, 2008; Davíð Ólafsson, 'Post-medieval manuscript culture and the historiography of texts,' *Mirrors of virtue: Manuscript and print in late pre-modern Iceland.* Matthew J. Driscoll and Margrét Eggertsdóttir, eds. Bibliotheca Arnamagnæana XLIX. Opuscula XV (Copenhagen: Museum Tusculanums, 2017), 1–30. Egodocuments are hugely popular among Icelandic readers, often featuring among the bestsellers for each year. Icelanders have been said to have this literary form, and personal history in general, 'on the brain.'

10 Sigurður Gylfi Magnússon, *Menntun, ást og sorg. Einsögurannsókn á íslensku sveitasamfélagi 19. og 20. aldar.* [Education, love and grief]. Sagnfræðirannsóknir 13 (Reykjavík: Háskólaútgáfan, 1997, 265–286; Jón Karl Helgason, *Hetjan og höfundurinn. Brot úr menningarsögu* [The Hero and the author] (Reykjavík: Mál og menning, 1998).

11 Sigurður Gylfi Magnússon, *Wasteland with Words.*

12 For some time now ethnologist Jón Jónsson has been researching the role of vagabonds in Icelandic life. See Jón Jónsson, *Á mörkum mennskunar* [On the brink of humanity]: *Sögur af förufólki í íslenska sveitasamfélaginu.* Sýnisbók íslenskrar alþýðumenningar 23 (Reykjavík: Háskólaútgáfan, 2018).

13 Sigurður Gylfi Magnússon and Davíð Ólafsson, *Minor Knowledge and Microhistory. Manuscript Culture in the Nineteenth Century* (London: Routledge, 2017). See also: Sigurður Gylfi Magnússon, *Wasteland with Words*; Guðný Hallgrímsdóttir, *A Tale of a Fool? A Microhistory of an 18th-Century Peasant Woman.* Microhistories. (London: Routledge, 2019).

14 Jónas Jónasson, *Íslenskir þjóðhættir* [Icelandic Folkways]. 2nd ed. (Reykjavík: Jónas og Halldór Rafnar, 1945), 3–9; Magnús Gíslason, *Kvällsvaka. En isländsk kulturtradition belyst genom studier i bondebefolkningens vardagsliv och miljö under senare hälften av 1800-talet och början av 1900-talet* [The winter-eve-gathering]. Studia Ethnologica Upsaliensia 2 (Uppsalir: Upsala Universitet, 1977); Hjalti Hugason, 'Kristnir trúarhættir,' [Christian religious traditions] *Íslensk þjóðmenning* V. *Trúarhættir.* Frosti F. Jóhannsson, ed. (Reykjavík: Þjóðsaga, 1988), 75–339.

15 Sigurður Gylfi Magnússon, 'From Children's Point of View: Childhood in Nineteenth Century Iceland,' *Journal of Social History,* 29 (winter 1995), 295–323; Sigurður Gylfi Magnússon and Davíð Ólafsson, 'Barefoot Historians: Education in Iceland in the Modern Period,' *Writing Peasants. Studies on Peasant Literacy in Early Modern Northern Europe.* Klaus-Joachim Lorenzen-Schmidt and Bjørn Poulsen (eds.). (Århus: Landbohistorisk Selskab, 2002), 175–209.

16 Sigurður Gylfi Magnússon, *Emotional Experience and Microhistory. A Life Story of a Destitute Pauper Poet in the 19th Century.* Microhistories (London: Routledge, 2020).

17 In this context, see Ólafur F. Hjartar's overview of book publication in Iceland: 'Íslenzk bókaútgáfa 1887-1966,' [Icelandic book publishing] *Árbók Landsbókasafns Íslands* 24 (1967), 137–141; Ólafur Halldórsson, 'Skrifaðar bækur,' [Written books] *Íslensk þjóðmenning* VI. Frosti F. Jóhannesson, ed. (Reykjavík: Þjóðsaga, 1989), 57–89; Steingrímur Jónsson, 'Prentaðar bækur,' [Printed books] *Íslensk þjóðmenning* VI. Frosti F. Jóhannesson, ed. (Reykjavík: Þjóðsaga, 1989), 91–115.

18 Sigurður Gylfi Magnússon, 'From Children's Point of View: Childhood in Nineteenth Century Iceland,' 295–323.

19 See a good discussion of the importance of the narrative for historical inquiry: Thomas V. Cohen, *Roman Tales: A Reader's Guide to the Art of Microhistory.* Microhistories (London: Routledge, 2019).

20 See Davíð Ólafsson's discussion of the status of peasant culture in the following papers: Davíð Ólafsson, 'Scribal communities in Iceland: The case of Sighvatur Grímsson,' *White Field, Black Seeds: Nordic Literacy Practices in the Long Nineteenth Century,* Anna Kuismin and Matthew J.

Driscoll eds. (Helsinki: Finnish Literature Society, 2013), 40–49; Davíð Ólafsson and Ólafur Rastrick, 'Current Trends in Icelandic Cultural History: Practices, Products and Perspectives,' *Revue d'Histoire Nordique* 20 (2016), 155–182.

21 Many examples might be cited here, of which I mention two: Jaume Aurell, 'Making History by Contextualizing Oneself: Autobiography as Historiographical intervention,' *History and Theory* 54 (May 2015), 244–268; Jeremy Popkin, *History, Historians and Autobiography* (Chicago: University of Chicago Press, 2005); Jeremy Popkin, '"Egohistoire and Beyond": Contemporary French Historian-Autobiographers,' *French Historical Studies* 19 (Fall 1996), 1059-1083 and 1139-1167.

22 Jaume Aurell, 'Making History by Contextualizing Oneself,' 245–246.

23 Jaume Aurell, 'Making History by Contextualizing Oneself,' 248.

24 Jaume Aurell, 'Making History by Contextualizing Oneself,' 262.

25 Jaume Aurell, 'Making History by Contextualizing Oneself,' 264.

26 Jaume Aurell, 'Making History by Contextualizing Oneself,' 264.

27 See an interesting dialogue about 'history without documents' which relates to regions of the globe which were categorized as colonies, where sources were 'tainted' by the perspective of the overlords – the colonial powers – if any such sources in fact existed. See Farina Mir, 'Introduction. *AHR Roundtable*: The Archives of Decolonization,' *American Historical Review* 120:3 (June 2015), 844–950. Each of the following contributed a paper to the Roundtable: Caroline Elkins, Todd Shepard, Jordanna Bailkin, Sarah Abrevaya Stein, Omnia El Shakry and Reuben Neptune.

28 Antoinette Burton, 'Introduction: Archive Fever, Archive Stories,' *Archive Stories: Facts, Fictions, and the Writing of History*. Antoinette Burton, ed. (Durham: Duke University Press, 2005), 3.

29 Jennifer S. Milligan, '"What is an Archive?" in the History of Modern France,' *Archive Stories: Facts, Fictions, and the Writing of History*. Antoinette Burton, ed. (Durham: Duke University Press, 2005), 177. See also: Michel De Certeau's great paper on the 'Historiographical Operation' in his book *The Writing of History*, trans. Tom Conley (New York: Columbia University Press, 1992).

30 Much has been written about photography as a phenomenon, but probably the best-known such work is by Roland Barthes, *Camera Lucida. Reflections on Photography*. Trans. Richard Howard (New York: Hill and Wang, 1981). I also wish to mention a number of works by Australian-American cultural historian Geoffrey Batchen, which have influenced me considerably. See e.g. *Each Wild Idea. Writing, Photography, History* (Cambridge, Mass.: The MIT Press, 2001); *Burning with Desire. The Conception of Photography* (Cambridge, Mass.: The MIT Press, 1999).

31 Peter Fritzsche, 'The Archive and the German Nation,' *Archive Stories: Facts, Fictions, and the Writing of History*. Antoinette Burton ed. (Durham: Duke University Press, 2005), 186.

32 Jane Bennett, *Vibrant Matter: A Political Ecology of Things* (Durham: NC: Duke University Press, 2010).

33 See here the pioneering work on photographs from the 70s and 80s by John Berger, *Ways of Seeing* (London: Penguin Books, 1972) or John Tagg, *The Burden of Representation: Essays on Photographies and Histories* (Armherst: University of Massachusetts Press, 1988) who looked at the way objects in images coded information.

34 An interesting book explores this in the context of archaeology, *Archaeology and Photography. Time, Objectivity and Archive*. Lesley McFadyen and Dan Hicks eds. (London: Bloomsbury, 2020).

35 See: Finnur Jónasson, Sólveig Ólafsdóttir and Sigurður Gylfi Magnússon, *Híbýli fátæktar. Húsnæði og veraldleg gæði fátæks fólks á 19. öld og fram á 20. öld* [Homes of Poverty] Sýnisbók íslenskrar alþýðumenningar 24 (Reykjavík: Háskólaútgáfan, 2018), 183–236. The artist, Unnar Örn, used these photos in his exhibit called: 'On the specific contribution of Iceland and Icelandic society to history of imperfection: photos from Iceland 1930–1945 collected by Sigurður Guttormsson.' Reykjavík, Gallerí Ágúst 2009.

36 Sigurður Gylfi Magnússon and István M. Szijártó, *What is Microhistory?*

37 Peter Burke, *Eyewitnessing. The Uses of Images as Historical Evidence* (London: Reaktion Books, 2001), 14–15.

38 Niamh Moore, Andrea Salter, Liz Stanley and Maria Tamboukou, 'In other archives and beyond,' *The Archive Project: Archival Research in the Social Sciences* (London: Routledge, 2017), 3.

39 Niamh Moore, Andrea Salter, Liz Stanley and Maria Tamboukou, 'In other archives and beyond,' 4.

40 See e.g. a discussion in *American Historical Review* 2015: 'AHR Roundtable: The Archives of Decolonization,' *American Historical Review* 120:3 (June 2015), 844–895.

41 Niamh Moore, Andrea Salter, Liz Stanley and Maria Tamboukou, 'In other archives and beyond,' 9. The book cited is by Carolyn Steedman, *Dust* (Manchester: Manchester University Press, 2001).

42 Sigurður Gylfi Magnússon and István M. Szijártó, *What is Microhistory?* 76–159.

43 Antoinette Burton, 'Introduction,' 7–8.

44 Niamh Moore, Andrea Salter, Liz Stanley and Maria Tamboukou, 'In other archives and beyond,' 20.

45 Niamh Moore, Andrea Salter, Liz Stanley and Maria Tamboukou, 'In other archives and beyond,' 24–25.

46 See Arlette Farge, *The Allure of the Archive*, trans. Thomas Scott-Railton (New Haven: Yale University Press, [1989] 2015).

47 *Archive Stories. Facts, Fictions, and the Writing of History*. Antoinette Burton, ed. (Durham: Duke University Press, 2005).

48 Niamh Moore, Andrea Salter, Liz Stanley and Maria Tamboukou, 'In other archives and beyond,' 24.

49 The phenomenon 'documentarist' is explained clearly in the following paper: Joshua Kates, 'Document and Time,' *History and Theory* 53 (May 2014), 155–174.

50 See for example John Randolph, 'The Bakunin Family Archive,' *Archive Stories: Facts, Fictions, and the Writing of History*. Antoinette Burton, ed. (Durham: Duke University Press, 2005), 209–231.

51 See Michel Foucault, 'Different Spaces,' trans. Robert Hurley, in James D. Faubion, ed., *Essential Works of Foucault, 1954–1988*, vol. 2: *Aesthetics, Method, and Epistemology* (New York: The New Press, 1988), 175–185.

52 Nile Green, 'AHR Forum: The Waves of Heterotopia: Toward a Vernacular Intellectual History of the Indian Ocean,' *American Historical Review* 123:3 (June 2018), 849.

53 Nile Green, 'AHR Forum: The Waves of Heterotopia,' 849.
54 Ewa Domańska, 'Affirmative Humanities,' *History – Theory – Criticism* 1 (2018), 9.
55 Ewa Domańska, 'Affirmative Humanities,' 12–13.
56 See Rosa Braidotti, 'In Spite of the Times. The Postsecular Turn in Feminism,' *Theory, Culture and Society* 25:6 (2008), 1–24.
57 Ewa Domańska, 'Affirmative Humanities,' 17.
58 Ewa Domańska, 'Affirmative Humanities,' 18.
59 Ewa Domańska, 'Affirmative Humanities,' 22.
60 Ewa Domańska, 'Affirmative Humanities,' 23.
61 See discussion of historians' autobiographical approach e.g. in Jaume Aurell's paper, cited above: 'Making History by Contextualizing Oneself,' Also an analysis of historians' autobiographies: Jeremy Popkin, *History, Historians, and Autobiography.*

Acknowledgments

I hereby acknowledge that the project was partly funded by the Icelandic Research Fund – IRF 184976-051 (in Icelandic: *Rannsóknasjóður*) – a Grant of Excellence for the project 'My Favourite Things: Material Culture Archives, Cultural Heritage and Meaning,' where I am the principal investigator (PI – see: http://hh.hi.is). I am grateful for the Fund's support for this three-year project. It has been a stimulating and satisfying intellectual experience to work with the talented and diverse set of people who were part of this research group.

The project is situated on an intersection between Material Culture Studies, History, and Museum and Archival Studies. The focus of the research is twofold: Firstly, emphasis is put on exploring the phenomenon of an 'archive'; how an image of the past is preserved and how people and their material environs are documented in different historical sources. Secondly, focus has been on how the 'archive' as a source has been employed in research within humanities and social sciences. Here we asked, what things did people own according to different archives, and how were they used? How did people relate to things, what was their value and their everyday significance? Different archives of material culture were juxtaposed, thus revealing opportunities to scrutinize the various ideas about the past from a new perspective, and simultaneously providing a new foundation for reviewing academics and scholarship. This is something I have tried to do in this book, and to my friends in the project – both Icelandic and from abroad – I say: many thanks for your generosity and intelligence.

The extraordinary friendship of many colleagues around the world with whom I have been in touch, first through the Reykjavík Academy and the Center for Microhistorical Research, and later both at the National Museum of Iceland, where I served as a senior researcher for three years, and finally at the University of Iceland, has affected the development of my thinking a great deal. I would like to thank them all for their amazing support and willingness to form an opinion of my ideas and thoughts.

I would also like to express my gratitude to my specialist in the English language – Anna Yates – who helped with this book; editing parts of it, reworking and translating some of the text. It has been extremely valuable for me to have access to her expertise, a specialist who has shown my work, in this book and others published in recent years, both interest and understanding.

I also wish to thank my friends and colleagues of many years' standing, Davíð Ólafsson, Assistant Professor of Cultural Studies in the School of Humanities, Faculty of Icelandic and Comparative Cultural Studies at the University of Iceland, Dr. Kristján Mímisson, archeologist at the University of Iceland, Prof. Gavin Murray Lucas, archeologist at the University of Iceland, and my doctoral students – Anna Heiða Baldursdóttir and Sólveig Ólafsdóttir – all of whom have enriched the project in so many ways. I would also like to thank the editors of Routledge for their cooperation and support throughout the years, especially Max Novick for his insight and constructive criticism.

I have been working on this project in recent years both as a professor of cultural history at the Department of History, University of Iceland, and as a visiting scholar at the University of California, Santa Barbara, USA, 2016–2017. I am grateful for all the support I have received from colleagues on both sides of the Atlantic in the development of this book.

Finally, I would like to take the opportunity to express my thanks to those who are closest to me and have been with me over the course of the last decades – my wife, Tinna Laufey Ásgeirsdóttir, a professor of economics at the University of Iceland, and my stepson, Pétur Bjarni, who now is approaching life as an adult, both of whom have been a constant inspiration for me. I will never be able to fully thank them for their love and support throughout the years. They have been an endless source of strength and encouragement. The book is dedicated to them.

Bibliography

Archival material

Letter from Magnús Helgason to Sigurður Gylfi Magnússon, written in Reykjavík, 28 September 1992. – Private archive.
Photographic collection of Helgi Magnússon. – Private archive.

Published works

Amelang, James S., 'Vox Populi: Popular Autobiographies as Sources for Early Modern Urban History,' *Urban History* 20 (1993), 30–42.
Appuhn, Karl, 'Microhistory,' *The Encyclopaedia of European Social History*, I. Peter N. Stearns, ed. (New York: Charles Scribners & Sons, 2001), 105–112.
Archive Stories. Facts, Fictions, and the Writing of History. Antoinette Burton ed. (Durham, Duke University Press, 2005).
Ash, Timothy Garton, *The File. A Personal History* (New York: Atlantic Books, 1997).
Aurell, Jaume, 'Making History by Contextualizing Oneself: Autobiography as Historiographical intervention,' *History and Theory* 54 (May 2015), 244–268.
'AHR Roundtable: The Archives of Decolonization,' *American Historical Review* 120:3 (June 2015), 844–895.
Baggerman, Arianne, 'Autobiography and Family Memory in the Nineteenth Century,' *Egodocuments and History. Autobiographical Writing in its Social Context since the Middle Ages.* Rudolf M. Dekker, ed. (Hilversum: Verloren, 2002), 161–175.
Barthes, Roland, *Camera Lucida. Reflections on Photography.* Trans. Richard Howard (New York: Hill and Wang, 1981).
Batchen, Geoffrey, *Each Wild Idea. Writing, Photography, History* (Cambridge, Mass.: The MIT Press, 2001).
Batchen, Geoffrey, *Burning with Desire. The Conception of Photography* (Cambridge, Mass.: The MIT Press, 1999).
Bell, Michael and Sze Tsung Leong, eds. *Slow Space* (New York: Monacelli Press, 1998).

Bender, Thomas A., 'Wholes and Parts: The Need for Synthesis in American History,' *Journal of American History* 73 (June 1986), 120–135.

Bender, Thomas, '"Venturesome and Cautious": American History in the 1990s,' *Journal of American History* 81 (December 1994), 992–1003.

Bennett, Jane, *Vibrant Matter: A Political Ecology of Things* (Durham, NC: Duke University Press, 2010).

Berger, John, *Ways of Seeing* (London: Penguin Books, 1972).

Birkiland, Jóhannes, *Harmsaga ævi minnar. Hvers vegna ég varð auðnuleysingi* (Reykjavík: Höfundur, 1945).

Braidotti, Rosa, 'In Spite of the Times. The Postsecular Turn in Feminism,' *Theory, Culture and Society* 25:6 (2008), 1–24.

Brown, Richard D., 'Microhistory and the Post-Modern Challenge,' *Journal of the Early Republic* 23:1 (2003), 1–20.

Brooks, James F., Christopher R.N. DeCorse, and John Walton, eds., *Small Worlds. Method, Meaning and Narrative in Microhistory* (Santa Fe: School for Advanced Research Press, 2008).

Brooks, Linda Marie, ed. *Alternative Identities. The Self in Literature, History, Theory* (New York: Routledge, 1995).

Burke, Peter, *The Fortunes of the Courtier: The European Reception of Castiglione's Cortegiano*, Penn State Series in the History of the Book (New York: Pennsylvania State University Press, 1996).

Burke, Peter, *Eyewitnessing. The Uses of Images as Historical Evidence* (London: Reaktion Books, 2001).

Burton, Antoinette, ed., 'Introduction: Archive Fever, Archive Stories,' *Archive Stories: Facts, Fictions, and the Writing of History* (Durham: Duke University Press, 2005).

Castrén, Anna-Maija, Karkku Lonkila, and Matti Peltonen, eds., *Between Sociology and History. Essays on Microhistory, Collective Action, and Nation-Building* (Helsinki: Suomalaisen kirjallisuuden seura, 2004).

Cohen, Thomas V., *Roman Tales: A Reader's Guide to the Art of Microhistory*. Microhistories (London: Routledge, 2019).

Conway, Jill Ker, *When Memory Speaks: Reflections on Autobiography* (New York: Alfred A. Knopf, Inc., 1998).

Conway, Mark A., *Theoretical Perspectives on Autobiographical Memory* (Dordrecht: Springer, 1992).

Couser, Thomas C. and Joseph Fichtelberg, eds. *True Relations. Essays on Autobiography and the Post-modern* (Westport, CT: Praeger, 1998).

Crane, Susan A., '*AHR Forum*: Writing the Individual Back into Collective Memory,' *American Historical Review* 102 (1997), 1372–1385.

Darian-Smith, Kate and Paula Hamilton, eds. *Memory and History in Twentieth-Century Australia* (Melbourne: Oxford University Press, 1994).

De Certeau, Michel, *The Writing of History*, Trans. Tom Conley (New York: Columbia University Press, 1992).

de Haan, Binne and Kostantin Mierau, eds., *Microhistory and the Picaresque Novel. A First Exploration into Commensurable Perspectives* (London: Cambridge Scholars Publishing, 2014).

Dekker, Rudolf M., *Childhood, Memory and Autobiography in Holland from Golden Age to Romanticism* (London: Palgrave, 1999).

Dekker, Rudolf M., ed. *Egodocuments and History. Autobiographical Writing in its Social Context since the Middle Ages* (Hilversum: Verloren, 2002).

Domańska, Ewa, 'Affirmative Humanities,' *History – Theory – Criticism*, 1 (2018), 9–26.

Dow, Timothy Adams, *Telling Lies in Modern American Autobiography* (Chapel Hill: University of North Carolina Press, 1990).

Egan, Susanna, *Mirror Talk. Genres of Crisis in Contemporary Autobiography* (Chapel Hill: University of North Carolina Press, 1999).

Farge, Arlette, *The Allure of the Archive*, Trans. Thomas Scott-Railton (New Haven: Yale University Press, [1989] 2015).

Folkenflik, Robert, ed. *The Culture of Autobiography: Constructions of Self-Representation* (Stanford: Stanford University Press, 1993).

Foucault, Michel, 'Different Spaces,' Trans. Robert Hurley, in James D. Faubion, ed., *Essential Works of Foucault, 1954–1988*, vol. 2: *Aesthetics, Method, and Epistemology* (New York: The New Press, 1988), 175–185.

Fredrickson, George M., 'Commentary on Thomas Bender's Call for Synthesis in American History,' *Reconstructing American Literary and Historical Studies.* Günther Lenz, Harmut Keil, and Sabine Bröck-Sallah, eds. (New York: Palgrave Macmillan, 1990), 74–81.

Fritzsche, Peter, 'The Archive and the German Nation,' *Archive Stories: Facts, Fictions, and the Writing of History.* Antoinette Burton, ed. (Durham, NC: Duke University Press, 2005).

Genette, Gérard, *Paratexts: Thresholds of Interpretation*, trans. Jane E. Lewin (Cambridge: Cambridge University Press, 1997).

Gilmore, Leigh, *The Limits of Autobiography. Trauma and Testimony* (Ithaca: Cornell University Press, 2001).

Ginzburg, Carlo, 'Clues: Roots of an Evidential Paradigm,' *Clues, Myths, and the Historical Method.* Trans. John and Anne Tedeschi (Baltimore: Johns Hopkins University Press, 1989), 96–125.

Ginzburg, Carlo, 'Microhistory and world history,' *The Cambridge World History.* Jerry H. Bentley, Sanjay Subrahmanyam and Merry E. Wiesner-Hanks, eds. (London: Cambridge University Press, 2015), 446–473.

Gíslason, Magnús, *Kvällsvaka. En isländsk kulturtradition belyst genom studier if bondebefolkningens vardagsliv och miljö under senare hälften av 1800-talet och början av 1900-talet.* Studia Ethnologica Upsaliensia 2 (Uppsalir: Upsala Universitet, 1977).

Graff, Harvey J., 'History's War of the Wor(l)ds,' *Sögustríð. Greinar og frásagnir um hugmyndafræði* (Reykjavík: Miðstöð einsögurannsókna and ReykjavíkurAkademían, 2007), 475–481.

Green, Nile, 'AHR Forum: The Waves of Heterotopia: Toward a Vernacular Intellectual History of the Indian Ocean,' *American Historical Review* 123:3 (June 2018), 846–874.

Gregory, Brad S., 'Is Small Beautiful? Microhistory and the Writing of Everyday Life,' Review essay in *History and Theory* 38:1(1999), 100–110.

'Gleðin var gríma. Viðtal við Kristínu Snæfells,' *Séð og heyrt* 12 (March 2003).

Gullestad, Marianne, ed. *Imagined Childhoods. Self and Society in Autobiographical Accounts* (Oslo: Scandinavian University Press, 1996).

Halbwachs, Maurice, *On Collective Memory* (Chicago: University of Chicago Press, 1992 [1914]).

Halldórsson, Ólafur, 'Skrifaðar bækur,' *Íslensk þjóðmenning* VI. Frosti F. Jóhannsson, ed. (Reykjavík: Þjóðsaga, 1989), 57–89.

Hallgrímsdóttir, Guðný, *A Tale of a Fool? A Microhistory of an 18th-Century Peasant Woman.* Microhistories (London: Routledge, 2019).

Hamerow, Theodore S., 'The Bureaucratization of History,' *American Historical Review* 94 (June 1989), 654–660.

Harlan, David, 'Intellectual History and the Return of Literature,' *American Historical Review* 94 (June 1989), 581–609.

Harlan, David, 'Reply to David Hollinger,' *American Historical Review* 94 (June 1989), 622–626.

Helgason, Jón Karl, 'Þýðing, endurritun, ritstuldur: Ort í eyður *Fortíðardrauma*,' *Íslensk menning*, vol. II: *Til heiðurs Sigurði Gylfa Magnússyni fimmtugum* (Reykjavík: Einsögustofnunin, 2007).

Helgason, Jón Karl, *Hetjan og höfundurinn. Brot úr menningarsögu* (Reykjavík: Mál og menning, 1998).

Helgason, Þröstur, 'Lífið er svört skáldsaga: Viðtal við José Saramago,' *Morgunblaðið* 11 September 2003.

Helgason, Þröstur, *Birgir Andrésson: Í íslenskum litum* (Reykjavík: Crymogea, 2010).

Himmelfarb, Gertrude, 'Some Reflections on the New History,' *American Historical Review* 94 (June 1989), 661–670.

Hjartar, Ólafur F., 'Íslenzk bókaútgáfa 1887–1966,' *Árbók Landsbókasafns Íslands* 24 (1967), 137–141.

Hoffman, Eva, *Lost in Translation. A Life in a New Language* (London: Penguin Books, 1989).

Hollinger, David, 'The Return of the Prodigal: the Persistence of Historical Knowing,' *American Historical Review* 94 (1989), 610–621.

Hugason, Hjalti, 'Kristnir trúarhættir,' *Íslensk þjóðmenning V. Trúarhættir.* Frosti F. Jóhannsson, ed. (Reykjavík: Þjóðsaga, 1988), 75–339.

Iggers, Georg G., *Historiography in the Twentieth Century: from Scientific Objectivity to the Postmodern Challenge* (Hanover, NH: Wesleyan University Press, 1997).

Jenkins, Keith, *Re-thinking History* (London: Routledge, 1991).

Jolly, Margaretta, ed. *Encyclopedia of Life Writing. Autobiographical and Biographical Forms* I-II (London: Routledge, 2002).

Jónasson, Finnur, Sólveig Ólafsdóttir and Sigurður Gylfi Magnússon, *Híbýli fátæktar. Húsnæði og veraldleg gæði fátæks fólks á 19. öld og fram á 20. öld* [Homes of Poverty] Sýnisbók íslenskrar alþýðumenningar 24 (Reykjavík: Háskólaútgáfan, 2018).

Jónsson, Jón, *Á mörkum mennskunar. Sögur af förufólki í íslenska sveitasamfélag-inu.* Sýnisbók íslenskrar alþýðumenningar 23 (Reykjavík: Háskólaútgáfan, 2018).

150   *Bibliography*

Jónasson, Jónas, *Íslenskir þjóðhættir*. 2nd ed. (Reykjavík: Jónas og Halldór Rafnar, 1945).

Jónsson, Steingrímur, 'Prentaðar bækur,' *Íslensk þjóðmenning* VI. Frosti F. Jóhannsson, ed. (Reykjavík: Þjóðsaga, 1989), 91–115.

Kates, Joshua, 'Document and Time,' *History and Theory* 53 (2014), 155–174.

Leask, Phil, *Friendship Without Borders. Women's Stories of Power, Politics, and Everyday Life across East and West Germany* (New York: Berghahn, 2020).

Lebert, Stephan and Norbert Lebert, *My Father's Keeper. The Children of the Nazi Leaders – An Intimate History of Damage and Denial*, Trans. Julian Evans (London: Back Bay Books, 2001).

Levine, Lawrence W., 'The Unpredictable Past: Reflections on Recent American Historiography,' *American Historical Review* 94 (1989), 671–679.

Levine, Robert, *A Geography of Time. The Temporal Misadventures of a Social Psychologist, or How Every Culture Keeps Time Just a Little Bit Differently* (New York: Basic Books, 1997).

Magnússon, Sigurður Gylfi, *Lífshættir í Reykjavík, 1930–1940*. Sagnfræðirannsóknir 7 (Reykjavík: Bókaútgáfa Menningarsjóðs, 1985).

Magnússon Sigurður Gylfi, 'From Children's Point of View: Childhood in Nineteenth Century Iceland,' *Journal of Social History* 29 (1995), 295–323.

Magnússon, Sigurður Gylfi, 'Kynjasögur á 19. og 20. öld? Hlutverkaskipan í íslensku samfélagi,' *Saga* 35 (1997), 137–177.

Magnússon, Sigurður Gylfi, *Menntun, ást og sorg. Einsögurannsókn á íslensku sveitasamfélagi 19. og 20. aldar*. Sagnfræðirannsóknir 13 (Reykjavík: Háskólaútgáfan, 1997).

Magnússon, Sigurður Gylfi, 'Sársaukans land. Vesturheimsferðir og íslensk hugsun,' *Burt – og meir en bæjarleið. Dagbækur og persónuleg skrif Vesturheimsfara á síðari hluta 19. aldar*. Sýnisbók íslenskrar alþýðumenningar 5. Davíð Ólafsson and Sigurður Gylfi Magnússon, eds. (Reykjavík: Háskólaútgáfan, 2001), 9–69.

Magnússon, Sigurður Gylfi and Davíð Ólafsson, 'Barefoot Historians: Education in Iceland in the Modern Period,' *Writing Peasants. Studies on Peasant Literacy in Early Modern Northern Europe*. Klaus-Joachim Lorenzen-Schmidt and Bjørn Poulsen, eds. (Århus: Landbohistorisk Selskab, 2002), 175–209.

Magnússon, Sigurður Gylfi, '*The Singularization of History:* Social History and Microhistory within the Postmodern State of Knowledge,' *Journal of Social History* 36 (Spring 2003), 701–735.

Magnússon, Sigurður Gylfi, *Fortíðardraumar. Sjálfsbókmenntir á Íslandi*. Sýnisbók íslenskrar alþýðumenningar 9 (Reykjavík: Háskólaútgáfan, 2004).

Magnússon, Sigurður Gylfi, *Snöggir blettir* (Reykjavík: Miðstöð einsögurannsókna and Ljósmyndasafn Reykjavíkur, 2004).

Magnússon, Sigurður Gylfi, *Sjálfssögur. Minni, minningar og saga*. Sýnisbók íslenskrar alþýðumenningar 11 (Reykjavík: Háskólaútgáfan, 2005).

Magnússon, Sigurður Gylfi, 'Social History as "Sites of Memory"? The Institutionalization of History: Microhistory and the Grand Narrative,' *Journal of Social History* Special issue 39:3 (Spring 2006), 891–913.

Magnússon, Sigurður Gylfi, *Sögustríð: Greinar og frásagnir um hugmyndafræði* (Reykjavík: Miðstöð einsögurannsókna and ReykjavíkurAkademían, 2007).

Magnússon, Sigurður Gylfi, *Wasteland with Words. A Social History of Iceland* (London: Reaktion books, 2010).

Magnússon, Sigurður Gylfi, and István M. Szijártó, *What is Microhistory? Theory and Practice* (London: Routledge, 2013).

Magnússon, Sigurður Gylfi, 'Living by the Book: Form, Text, and Life Experience in Iceland,' *White Field, Black Seeds: Nordic Literacy Practices in the Long Nineteenth Century*. Matthew James Driscoll and Anna Kuismin, eds. (Helsinki: Finnish Literature Society, 2013), 53–62.

Magnússon, Sigurður Gylfi, 'Gender: A Useful Category in Analysis of Ego-Documents? Memory, Historical Sources and Microhistory,' *Scandinavian Journal of History* 38:2 (2013), 202–222.

Magnússon, Sigurður Gylfi, 'Tales of the Unexpected: The "Textual Environment," Ego-Documents and a Nineteenth-Century Icelandic Love Story – An Approach in Microhistory,' *Cultural and Social History* 12:1 (2015), 77–94.

Magnússon, Sigurður Gylfi, 'The Love Game as Expressed in Ego-Documents: The Culture of Emotions in Late Nineteenth Century Iceland,' *Journal of Social History* 50:1 (2016), 102–119.

Magnússon, Sigurður Gylfi, 'Views into the Fragments: An Approach from a Microhistorical Perspective,' *International Journal of Historical Archaeology* 20 (2016), 182–206.

Magnússon, Sigurður Gylfi, 'Microhistory, Biography and Ego-Documents in Historical Writing,' *Revue d'histoire Nordique* 20 (2016), 133–153.

Magnússon, Sigurður Gylfi, 'Far-Reaching Microhistory: The Use of Microhistorical Perspective in a Globalized World,' *Rethinking History* 21:3 (2017), 312–341.

Magnússon, Sigurður Gylfi and Davíð Ólafsson, *Minor Knowledge and Microhistory. Manuscript Culture in the Nineteenth Century* (London: Routledge, 2017).

Magnússon, Sigurður Gylfi, *Emotional Experience and Microhistory. A Life Story of a Destitute Pauper Poet in the 19th Century*. Microhistories (London: Routledge, 2020).

Magnússon, Sigurður Gylfi, 'At the Mercy of Emotions: Archives, Egodocuments and Microhistory,' *The Routledge History of Emotions in the Modern World*. Katie Barclay and Peter N. Stearns, eds. (London: Routledge, 2022), forthcoming.

Mascuch, Michael, Rudolf Dekker, Arianne Baggerman, 'Egodocuments and History,' *The Historian* 78:1 (2016), 11–56.

McCullagh, C. Behan, 'Bias in Historical Description, Interpretation, and Explanation,' *History and Theory* 39 (February 2000), 39–66.

McFadyen, Lesley and Dan Hicks, eds., *Archaeology and Photography. Time, Objectivity and Archive* (London: Bloomsbury, 2020).

McKenzie, Don, *Bibliography and the Sociology of Texts* (London: Cambridge University Press, 1986).

152   Bibliography

Megill, Allan, 'Recounting the Past: Description, Explanation, and Narrative in Historiography,' *American Historical Review* 94 (June 1989), 627–653.

Milligan, Jennifer S., '"What is an Archive?" in the History of Modern France?' *Archive Stories: Facts, Fictions, and the Writing of History*. Antoinette Burton, ed. (Durham, Duke University Press, 2005).

Mir, Farina, 'Introduction. *AHR Roundtable*: The Archives of Decolonization,' *American Historical Review* 120:3 (June 2015), 844–950.

Mímisson, Kristján and Sigurður Gylfi Magnússon, 'Singularizing the Past: The History and Archaeology of the Small and Ordinary,' *Journal of Social Archaeology* 14:2 (2014), 131–156.

Monkkonen, Eric H., 'The Dangers of Synthesis,' *American Historical Review*, 91 (December 1986), 1146–1157.

Moore, Niamh, Andrea Salter, Liz Stanley and Maria Tamboukou, 'In Other Archives and Beyond,' *The Archive Project: Archival Research in the Social Sciences* (London, Routledge, 2017).

Munslow, Alun, *The Future of History* (London: Palgrave Macmillan, 2010).

Munslow, Alun, *Deconstructing History* (London: Routledge, 1997).

Murakami, Haruki, *Underground. The Tokyo Gas Attack and the Japanese Psyche*. Trans. Alfred Birnbaum and Philip Gabriel (London: Vintage, 2000).

Nora, Pierre, 'Between Memory and History: *Les Lieux de Mémoire*.' *Representations* 26 (Spring 1989), 7–25.

Olábarri, Ignacio, '"New" New History: a *Longue Durée* Structure,' *History and Theory* 34 (1995), 1–29.

Ólafsson, Davíð, 'Wordmongers: Post-Medieval Scribal Culture and the Case of Sighvatur Grímsson,' PhD diss., University of St. Andrews, 2008.

Ólafsson, Davíð, 'Scribal Communities in Iceland: The Case of Sighvatur Grímsson,' *White Field, Black Seeds: Nordic Literacy Practices in the Long Nineteenth Century*, Anna Kuismin and Matthew J. Driscoll, eds. (Helsinki: Finnish Literature Society, 2013), 40–49.

Ólafsson, Davíð and Ólafur Rastrick, 'Current Trends in Icelandic Cultural History: Practices, Products and Perspectives,' *Revue d'Histoire Nordique* 20 (2016), 155–182.

Ólafsson, Davíð, 'Post-medieval Manuscript Culture and the Historiography of Texts,' *Mirrors of virtue: Manuscript and print in late pre-modern Iceland*. Matthew J. Driscoll and Margrét Eggertsdóttir, eds. Bibliotheca Arnamagnæana XLIX. Opuscula XV (Copenhagen: Museum Tusculanums, 2017), 1–30.

Ólafsson, Ragnar Helgi, *Bókasafn föður míns. Sálumessa (samtíningur)*. (Reykjavík: Bjartur, 2018).

Olney, James, '(Auto) biography,' *Southern Review* 22 (1986), 428–441.

Peltonen, Matti, 'Clues, Margins and Monads. The Micro-Macro Link in Historical Research,' *History and Theory* 40 (2001), 347–359.

Pieters, Jürgen, 'New Historicism: Postmodern Historiography between Narrativism and Heterology,' *History and Theory* 39 (February 2000), 21–38.

Popkin, Jeremy, *History, Historians and Autobiography* (Chicago, IL: University of Chicago Press, 2005).

Popkin, Jeremy, "'Ego-histoire and Beyond": Contemporary French Historian-Autobiographers,' *French Historical Studies* 19 (Fall 1996), 1059–1083 and 1139–1167.

Putnam, Lara, 'To Study the Fragments/Whole: Microhistory and the Atlantic World,' *Journal of Social History* 39:3 (2006), 615–630.

Randolph, John, 'The Bakunin Family Archive,' *Archive Stories: Facts, Fictions, and the Writing of History*. Antoinette Burton, ed. (Durham: Duke University Press, 2005), 209–231.

Richardson, Brian, *Print Culture in Renaissance Italy: The Editor and the Vernacular Text, 1470–1600* (Cambridge: Cambridge University Press, 1994).

Ross, Bruce M., *Remembering the Personal Past. Descriptions of Autobiographical Memory* (New York: Oxford University Press, 1991).

Roth, Michael S., *The Ironist's Cage: Memory, Trauma and the Construction of History* (New York: Columbia University Press, 1995).

Rubin, David C., *Remembering Our Past: Studies in Autobiographical Memory* (Cambridge: Cambridge University Press, 1996).

Scott, Joan Wallach, 'History in Crisis? The Others' Side of the Story,' *American Historical Review* 94 (June 1989), 680–692.

Simon, Zoltán Boldizsár, 'Microhistory: In General,' *Journal of Social History* 49:1 (2015), 237–248.

Smith, Sidonie and Julia Watson, eds. *Getting a Life. Everyday Uses of Autobiography* (Minneapolis: University of Minnesota Press, 1996).

Stearns, Peter N., 'Debates About Social History and its Scope,' *Sögustríð. Greinar og frásagnir um hugmyndafræði* (Reykjavík: Miðstöð einsögurannsókna and ReykjavíkurAkademían, 2007), 17–21.

Stearns, Peter N., 'Social History and History: A Progress Report,' *Journal of Social History*, 19 (Winter 1985), 319–334.

Steedman, Carolyn, *Dust* (Manchester: Manchester University Press, 2001).

Steedman, Carolyn, *Past Tenses. Essays on Writing Autobiography and History* (London: Rivers Oram Press, 1992).

Stengers, Isabelle, *Another Science is Possible. A Manifesto for Slow Science*, Trans. Stephen Muecke (London: Polity, 2018).

Szijártó, István M., 'Four Arguments for Microhistory,' *Rethinking History* 6:2 (2002), 209–215.

Tagg, John, *The Burden of Representation: Essays on Photographies and Histories* (Armherst: University of Massachusetts Press, 1988).

Thelen, David, Nell Irvin Painter, Richard Wightman Fox, Roy Rosenzweig and Thomas Bender, 'A Round Table: Synthesis in American History,' *Journal of American History*, 74 (June 1987), 107–130.

Tilly, Charles, *Big Structures, Large Processes, Huge Comparisons* (New York: Russell Sage Foundation, 1984).

Toews, John E., 'Perspectives on "The Old History and the New": A Comment,' *American Historical Review* 94 (June 1989), 693–698.

Trivellato, Francesca, 'Is There a Future for Italian Microhistory in the Age of Global History?' *California Italian Studies* 2:1 (2011): http://escholarship.org/uc/item/0z94n9hq.

Trivellato, Francesca, 'Microhistoria/Microhistorie/Microhistory,' *French Politics, Culture and Society* 33:1 (2015), 122–134.

White, Louis, *Speaking with Vampires. Rumor and History in Colonial Africa* (California: University of California Press, 2000).

Wood, Nancy, *Vectors of Memory. Legacies of Trauma in Postwar Europe* (Oxford: Berg Publishers, 1999).

Index